John Bentley
My Story

JOHN BENTLEY

My Story

John Bentley with Neil Squires

André Deutsch

First published in 1999
by André Deutsch Limited
76 Dean Street
London W1V 5HA

www.vci.co.uk

A catalogue record for this book is available from the British Library

ISBN 0 233 99424 6

Plate section design
by Design 23

Typeset by
Derek Doyle & Associates, Liverpool
Printed and bound in Great Britain by
Mackays of Chatham

To the memory of the gentle giant of rugby league,
friend to so many, Roy Powell

Acknowledgements

My thanks go to: Neil Squires for a fantastic job writing this book, and for not losing his cool when told we were 35,000 words short with three weeks to deadline. To Mal Reilly and Fran Cotton, two men who influenced the course of my career, for their forewords. To Tim Forrester at André Deutsch for commissioning the book, despite his own life being thrown into turmoil by the demise of Richmond RU. Also to Ingrid Connell, Kerrin Edwards and all concerned for their enthusiasm, commitment and dedication to making the book a success.

Thanks to the *Newcastle Chronicle, Yorkshire Post* and the *Halifax Evening Courier* for their cooperation with the photographs. And to Ray Fletcher and John Ledger for their help with the statistics.

Thanks to all who have assisted me, and there are many, in any shape or form, be it coaching or advice, throughout the course of my life and career.

To Mum and Dad and sister Sarah, for guiding me through the early challenging years. And finally thanks to Sandy, my wife, for providing the love and support which has provided the foundation of everything I have achieved. Love to son Lloyd and daughters Faye and Millie.

Contents

Forewords by Fran Cotton and Malcolm Reilly	xi
Introduction	1
Chapter One	11
Chapter Two	23
Chapter Three	43
Chapter Four	55
Chapter Five	83
Chapter Six	97
Chapter Seven	117
Chapter Eight	139
Chapter Nine	161
Chapter Ten	181
Chapter Eleven	205
Chapter Twelve	223
Epilogue	233
Appendix	235
Index	237

Forewords

··

Rugby, more so than any other sport, is full of larger than life characters. 'Bentos' fits into that category.

I have always enjoyed and admired his rugby skills from a young player through to his many achievements both in rugby union and rugby league. Above all else, I will remember his sense of fun and mischievousness. When 'Bentos' was around, life was never dull.

On occasions the fun element has overshadowed the rugby, notably on the England tour to Australia in 1988. He was a young man enjoying life to the full but not mature enough to balance work and play. What a difference ten years in the hard school of rugby league made!

'Bentos' was a surprise choice for the 1997 British Lions tour to South Africa, having returned to rugby union the same season. I was always confident of his rugby ability and the positive contribution his personality would make to team spirit. He didn't disappoint and had a marvellous tour. He made the test team, scored spectacular tries, was the supporters' hero and kept everybody amused. That was the 1997 'Bentos' who worked hard at his game and enjoyed the experience.

I feel privileged to have been asked to write this foreword and doubly privileged to have enjoyed his company both as a player and a man. Good luck, John, to you and your family.

Fran Cotton

I feel fortunate to have had over the years an association with John, from the onset signing him on professional forms for Leeds and later coaching him at Halifax.

Every team needs a John Bentley. First and foremost, his attitude is what stands out and his determined approach in the pursuit of success.

John achieved dual international status, which in itself is a great accomplishment. Firstly playing for England against France in rugby league and later playing an outstanding role in the British Lions' success in South Africa. I was so pleased that he made his mark at the very highest level. It is a just reward for his enthusiasm and determination.

John is an inspiration both on and off the field. He leads from the front in training; extra effort is his trademark in preparing himself for the contest ahead. He is a confident player and that confidence comes through his commitment. He has also got a great sense of humour. He just loves a bit of friendly fun with team mates, management or his coach – a real 'larrikin' as the Aussies would say.

His personality is also one of his strong points. A great communicator who doesn't mind calling a spade a spade, delicate issues have never been a problem for John Bentley to broach.

These qualities will, I am sure, be put to good use after he has stopped fighting for the extra yard carrying the ball. I am convinced that, in the not too distant future, coaching will be a natural avenue for John to pursue.

I wish him all the best in the future, particularly with this book. Thank you, John, for your efforts, your honesty and your friendship over the years.

Malcolm Reilly O.B.E.

Introduction

I never thought I would be allowed back. Having made the decision to go to rugby league, I knew the door was locked behind me. Union was amateur, league was professional, and never were the twain allowed to meet. It was hypocritical at a time when players were benefiting from inflated 'expenses' in rugby union but that was the way it was. One day I hoped to return to Cleckheaton, where I started out, and play social rugby union in the third team, perhaps under an assumed name. But the England team? No way.

In 1993 I had played in a Halifax rugby league side that included Steve Pilgrim, a former Wasps full-back who had been banned by the Rugby Football Union for a year for playing a trial match with the Leeds league side – for which he'd not even been paid. I had benefited in kind during my time in union and so had plenty of others but officially of course we were amateurs. Sale's travel expenses and Christmas bonuses never matched those of other big clubs but the money came in handy nonetheless. The joke went that the only difference between league and union was that you paid tax in league. If the RFU had bothered to find out what was going on we would all have been in big trouble but the powers-that-be buried

1

their heads in the sand and stored up massive problems for themselves when the tide finally came in.

Union finally went professional in August 1995 after Rupert Murdoch paid £360 million for the television rights to the southern hemisphere game. League, guided by the same satellite trappings, switched to summer the following year. In less than 12 months the bricks on which the two games had been built were swept away. The rugby world was turned on its head. In this new environment the barriers between the two codes of rugby had to come crashing down. They did. And nine years after my last England cap there I found myself in Sydney wearing that beautiful pristine white shirt again – only now it had black and red bands and a sponsor's name on it. Becoming the first rugby league player to return and play union for England was just the most wonderful, unimaginable treat.

The 1997 British Lions tour to South Africa finally drew a line under the days when people in rugby union looked down their noses at rugby league. The contribution made by the players who had returned from league left them with no choice. Because of my nine years in rugby league, I was in the odd position of being one of the oldest players on the tour but yet one of the most inexperienced at international level. There were some legends surrounding me – people like Jerry Guscott and Martin Johnson who had done it all in rugby union. In their presence I had the choice of being a wallflower or to speak up and try to get across what I had learned from life in the professional code. I chose the latter. The union lads had more to learn from me and the other rugby league boys in terms of attitude and approach than I had from them. They had giant strides to make in that department.

Our very first pre-tour training session at London Irish would be as intense as many of the union lads had seen. We were split into groups of six – each a mixture of forwards and backs. I was holding a tackle bag alongside Jason Leonard and Martin Johnson, the Lions' captain. While the players were working, moving back and forth smashing into tackle shields, I was shouting encouragement at them, urging them to imagine the bags were South Africans. I was trying to get them high and they responded. Jonno was laughing at me and telling me to calm down because it was 'only training'. I stopped. That was the point: it was *training* and the whole environment had to prepare us for the way we were going to play. I snapped at Jonno and told him this was the way it had to be if we were going to beat the South Africans. Scott Gibbs, Dai Young, Alan Tait, they were all challenging the players to give more because that was what we were used to in league.

After the session Jonno got the players together in a huddle. He told them I had set the standards of intensity which we were never going to drop below on the tour. We didn't. Professionalism isn't the job you do, it's the way you do the job and rugby union was just cottoning on to that. The league contingent helped fast-forward that process.

The receptiveness of the manager, Fran Cotton, and the coach, Ian McGeechan, to league influences was important to the success of that amazing tour. Not only in picking league players but in using techniques from the rival code. Their backgrounds were probably helpful in this respect as Fran's family played league in Lancashire and Geech used to teach in Leeds when he played for Yorkshire. He immediately recognized that the six of us who had been league professionals had something the Lions needed to take on board if they were to confound the odds in South Africa. He constantly picked our brains throughout the tour.

Those seven weeks in 1997 attracted league people back home who had never previously shown an interest in union. The presence of familiar players like myself and Scott Gibbs helped but some of the rugby we played was so good it appealed across the board. The Test matches might have held the drama and emotion but the game against Free State in Bloemfontein when we won 52–30 contained the most exceptional rugby I have been involved in at either code. Even the most dyed-in-the-wool league nut would have been hard pressed not to have enjoyed it, however much they tried.

The day before the dramatic Second Test victory which won the Lions the series, the squad received faxes from the technical director of the Rugby Football League, Joe Lydon, and Phil Larder, the former Great Britain coach who was later to be taken on board by England. They told us we had earned their respect and they wished us well in the game. In many ways that said more than the congratulatory message we received from Tony Blair after we had won in Durban. In it the prime minister said the team spirit we had so clearly fostered had proved priceless on the pitch. He was right and I like to think I played my part in creating it.

Before I went on the tour Newcastle's coach Steve Bates told me he didn't think I was up to it. I told him I would prove him wrong and I did. I might not be the most talented player to have handled a ball but I have always tried to make up for my deficiencies through hard work. If another player is more gifted I can admit it and then redouble my efforts to bridge that gap. I have a strong work ethic and I am a big believer in life giving you back what you put in. Perhaps what happened on that Lions tour, when I finished top try-scorer and ran in a really special touchdown against Gauteng, which helped put the tour back on track, was my reward.

Perversely, I always thought there was more chance of me playing for the British Lions than England on my return from rugby league. The Lions was a short-term operation sent out to South Africa to win, a mixture of nationalities and backgrounds. I always felt the establishment at the RFU would have blocked any move to pick a rugby league player for the English national side. In any case England should have been looking to the future and I was 30 when the call came second time around. Still, when it came I knew I was there on merit. The setting for my return was a familiar one.

I had played in the Sydney Football Stadium as a rugby league player in the World Sevens. The shirts were waiting in the changing rooms when we arrived. I looked at mine, then picked it up and kissed the rose. I had made it back.

Things had changed since I had last been there as an international rugby union player: this time it was serious. Playing for England in 1988 had been a great honour but also an excuse for some outrageous drinking feats and world-class larking about. Which was probably why I was picked. I am seen as a joker, someone who loves acting the goat and entertaining those around me. Sport is about characters and life as well as winning and losing and I hope I've been able to leave some part of mine behind at the places I have played. Any group needs its jokers, particularly a bunch of rugby players who are going through physical pain every weekend. A laugh now and again helps to lighten the load. I want to be liked by everyone, as most clowns do, but I can understand why I'm not everyone's cup of tea.

Sometimes, as on the field, I am unpredictable but I think

that is what people find entertaining about me. Like other, rather more renowned comedians, I can get very low sometimes – I did on the Lions tour when things weren't going right and I was a long way from home. I allow things to get on top of me, watching them pile up until I find myself right at the bottom. From that position there's only one way to go. So there are no half measures – I'm either on top of the world or locked away in the darkest of cellars.

I'm also told I am intimidating to be with. This isn't deliberate, it's just the way I am. Confident individuals can walk into a room and talk to anyone. One of my strengths is an ability to get along with a wide range of people. On that Lions tour there were 35 players and, despite all we tried to do to avoid it, that inevitably meant cliques. I could easily drift from one section to another, make conversation and be at ease – others couldn't. I even infiltrated the Welsh clan on that trip.

I suppose when it comes down to it I'm a show-off. There is a certain type of individual that I get on with best – easy-going types who aren't as demanding in terms of the limelight. With someone like Jerry Guscott it is an unwitting battle for attention with neither of us wanting to be outdone. Usually I can have a row with someone and forget it moments later but if they bear a grudge I will always get even, no matter how long it takes. That determination to settle scores permeates my rugby and has led to some rare old battles throughout my career – with Martin Offiah amongst others. Our relationship was one long row. Martin played opposite me which didn't help for a start and he didn't show me any respect either. I'm not a Martin Offiah – at the top of his game he was the best in the world – but I always got stuck into him when I played against him which is something people used to enjoy. He was a tremendous athlete and a gifted footballer who was also massively arrogant in his early days. But over time this mellowed, as did our dislike for each other. We were never bosom buddies but we could at least respect each other's different qualities.

I like to think my instincts about people and situations are largely accurate. I can weigh folk up pretty quickly. Will Carling for instance: for some reason I knew we'd never be friends. We came through at the same time in the same part of the country but from very different upbringings and we had a couple of titanic struggles when we were on the way up. He came a very distant second.

Ieuan Evans used to say on the Lions tour that I said what I liked and I liked what I said. I suppose he was right, really. I am an honest individual – what you see is what you get – and I don't mind giving forthright opinions. That has got me into trouble in the past but I can't change the way I am.

People say what a great life being a full-time sportsman is – and they're right – but for me the chaotic double life I used to lead suited me better. I have to be doing something all the time. Full-time professional rugby has been very hard work in this respect as it leaves you with so many spare hours in the day. For two thirds of my career I, like nearly every other rugby player of either code, was combining it with work. I would race home from a police shift, say hello to my wife and young family, and be off out of the door straight away to train or play.

A low boredom threshold can mean trouble for my team-mates. At every club I've been to there has tended to be a trail of pranks left behind. Team photographs are a heaven-sent opportunity for trouble. Many is the time that a family-friendly snap has been ruined by the appearance of my privates, peeking out from the side of my shorts. I can't claim to have invented this one as there is a shot of the appropriately named Leeds star of the 70s, Kevin Dick, on the wall of a pub in the city, with his decorations happily hanging out.

My favourite victim tended to be Huddersfield teammate Paul Loughlin who always sneaked off to the sunbed instead of doing some weight-training at the gym. The door to the sunbed room had an emergency lock which I worked out could be opened from the outside with a coin. I used to put my hand in, whip his clothes and hide them. He had to come out stark naked to find them, much to the public's surprise and his embarrassment. Having suffered this fate on about half a dozen occasions, 'Lockers' cottoned on that it might be a good idea to hide his clothes himself so I couldn't remove them. That was asking for trouble. I went outside into the car park and selected a nasty two-foot-long nettle from a clump. With my teammates looking on in horror I picked the lock again and threw the nettle into the sunbed and on to his groin area. Poor Lockers was thrashing about all over the place trying to get it off – it looked like he was in a bath with an electric heater. He was last seen searching the car park for dock leaves.

I've been involved with a few rugby clubs in my time. In union there were the amateur excesses of life with Cleckheaton, Otley and Sale, followed by a totally different experience on my return with the professional pioneers of Newcastle. That ended in tears as did my brief flirtation with Rotherham.

In league there were the great underachievers Leeds, where powerful personalities like Garry Schofield stamped their mark. Then there were six years at Halifax, engaging underdogs, who spent their way into trouble. And finally there was Huddersfield and a reunion with one of English rugby league's best coaches, Malcolm Reilly.

Although league and union are very different games – more different than many watchers imagine – they are both rugby and that attracts a certain type of person. The intense physical nature of both sports leaves no room for prima donnas – only people who are prepared to muck in for each other. I love that element in both games.

The similarities in the evolution of both sports in the 90s have been striking. Few games can have changed so much so quickly, and with such great risks. League alienated its traditional support by switching seasons; union did likewise by paying its players. The battle for control of English rugby union led to a bitter fight between the top clubs and the Rugby Football Union. At the same time a power struggle was going on in rugby league between the governing body and the clubs' body Super League Europe. Different codes, same problem. In the middle, as always, were the players. Here were two games attempting to come to terms with changes that threatened to tear them both apart.

I witnessed the revolutions from within and there was a lot of heartache involved for a lot of people. But while diehards from both codes were bemoaning the removal of the soul from their sports, I couldn't have been happier. The door was open again – and somebody was daft enough to pay me for going through it.

Chapter 1

I could have been a Springbok. I know, it's a shocking thought isn't it? In 1970, when I was almost four, the Bentley household moved lock, stock and barrel from impoverished Cleckheaton to the promised land of South Africa to set up a new home. Dad was a sheet-metal worker at the time and an opportunity arose for him to ply his trade in the dockyards out there. The temptation to abandon our terraced house in our close-knit street where everybody knew everybody else's business for the open spaces and freedom of Africa proved irresistible. The journey took 12 days on a boat called the Prince Orange, which can't have been much fun for Mum and Dad with a terror like me to look after and my little sister too. I was more mischievous than malicious but I just seemed to find myself at the heart of any interesting action. Some things don't change.

When we arrived in the republic we lived at first in a high-rise block of flats, which wasn't quite the image of South Africa we had been sold. Where were the endless plains? Having to climb all those steps made life tough for the local milkman but it was made even worse one day by the sight of his electric float disappearing into the distance with a four-year-old Yorkshireman at the wheel. It was joyriding in its most innocent form but Mum was not impressed. She employed a 'three warnings then a smack' policy which meant a regularly aching hand for her. Shoplifting was the next rap. I pinched a couple of sweets from the local shop, ate the first one but forgot about the second, a chocolate affair, which melted in my pocket. Mum found the remnants and marched me back to the shop to apologize.

There was more trouble when we moved to a lovely open-plan bungalow near the beach in Fish Hoek. This was more like it: a beautiful part of the world 20 miles from Cape Town with abundant opportunities for swimming, playing and causing chaos. We lived the outdoor life, taking advantage of the climate to follow the local custom of having barbecues all the time. The endless stretch of white sand on our doorstep was lapped by the Indian Ocean – home to some spectacularly large fish, particularly when all I had seen before was battered cod. When one careless fisherman's attention wandered I took the opportunity to steal his catch – a shark which was as big as me. I dragged the giant creature off towards Mum who was sitting on the rocks with some friends. Oddly she did not seem particularly grateful. Nor did the fisherman.

Life in South Africa for me was simple: it involved swimming and playing on the beach, where I learned to ride a bike because it didn't hurt when you fell off. For me hardship entailed losing my fingernail which I did on two occasions – once at the bottom of the pool on a loose tile and the other time when I trapped my hand in a deckchair. I was blissfully unaware of what others were going through in that divided country at the time. I went to an all-white school, took as read the fact that servants and menial workers were black and even picked up the disgusting language of apartheid.

And there was also a game called rugby. If you haven't been to the country, it is difficult to appreciate the importance placed on sport in general and rugby in particular by the white community. Whereas in England I would have been given a football at that age to play with, the natural thing in South Africa was to be bought a rugby ball. Sometimes the most important choices are made for you. During our two-year stay in the country my dad had the chance to see some top-class rugby, including the Springboks v. France. He brought me back a programme, which was the closest I came to seeing the legends in action until I ran into them head on 25 years later with the Lions.

A homesick Bentley clan cut short their South African adventure early and my mum recalls with acute embarrassment her son's behaviour on the boat back to Blighty. A black family was using the deck facilities and I apparently shouted out in my newly acquired South African accent that there was 'a kaffir in the pool'. The family was fine about it but I was given some urgent instructions on life in the real world in time for my arrival back in multicultural West Yorkshire. Years later I was accused by a journalist from the *Daily Telegraph* of making racist remarks against Ralph Knibbs, the black Bristol centre, during a John Player Cup quarter-final for Sale. I was outraged and told him in no uncertain terms how wrong he had been.

As a child my two great fears were Daleks and darkness and a combination of the two invariably led to nightmares. Saturday teatime back in England meant *Dr Who* and although I was petrified I used to put myself through the terrifying ritual each week. I used to wet the bed until I was eight and even as a supposed adult I have to check in all the cupboards in my house before turning the lights off, afraid of what might be lurking inside. I'm still scared of the dark. In my book a power cut is a lot more frightening than Jonah Lomu – especially if a high-pitched voice squawks *'Exterminate!'* in the middle of it.

I have always been a bit of a fighter, scrapping with friends mainly – or opposing wingers. I remember tripping up a girl called Caeron Case when I was little and breaking her collar-bone. I didn't mean to hurt her, it was an accident, but I was scared stiff because all the big girls came after me and it was only my speed which saved me from a beating. Caeron recovered sufficiently well to end up marrying Jim Mallinder, the Sale full-back who toured Argentina with England in 1997.

Although I could look after myself I was quite small for my age and I was bullied for a time at school. The misery and loneliness this caused made a deep impression. Even now, if I see someone on the receiving end, I will stick my nose in, whether it is wanted or not, because I know what it feels like. This one lad who made my life hell was massive. He used to make me queue up for his dinner tickets and if I refused he would hit me. I'd love to meet him again – preferably in a secluded alley. There was another kid who used to give me a hard time as well but a dust-up at The Frontier nightclub in Batley a few years on evened up that score.

My childhood was generally a happy time though (some of those close to me say it still is). I was up to all sorts – including giving my baby sister Sarah as hard a time as humanly possible. These days I would probably have been diagnosed as having attention deficit disorder but then I was just a hyper-active pain of a brother to have around – and cunning with it. Sarah, who is 19 months younger than I, used to fall for a game we called doggies every time. We each started off with a bag of sweets and I had to pretend to be a dog and perform tricks to win Sarah's off her. She was invariably left in tears with an empty bag.

Mum could not take me anywhere. Once, a friend of the family, Barbara Taylor, invited us in for a coffee and I disappeared into the kitchen while they had a chin wag. Barbara had been baking and when they came in to see what I was up to they discovered the dozen buns she had just made each had a single bite taken out of them.

Cigarettes were another temptation. I couldn't smoke but of course I would put a fag in my mouth and pretend to inhale like the rest of the lads on our street before wolfing down a pack of mints to hide the smell before I went home. I never smoked for real though.

When Dad found a new job the family moved out of my grandparents' house in Birkenshaw where we had been holed up since we arrived back from Africa and into a home of our own in nearby Liversedge. It wasn't a momentous move – both are small communities housed within the urban sprawl of West Yorkshire where one town merges into other. Liversedge and Birkenshaw are the sort of places you could blink and miss. The architecture isn't stunning, the streets aren't paved with gold, they are just places to live. There are no pretensions here. To the east lies flashy Leeds where accountants and wine bars predominate – the capital of the northern cappucino belt as it was recently described. We have more in common with Huddersfield, Halifax and Bradford – places which have all had to learn to get by as best they can after the decline of the woollen trade on which the local economy was based.

Nearby lies Batley, with its large Indian population, and through Heckmondwike, the Pakistani stronghold of Dewsbury. The Asian community arrived in droves after the war to work in the mills. They were already well established when I was growing up but not in the predominantly white, working-class parts where we found ourselves living. We had managed to move to a place that backed onto a green playing area which was quite an achievement in that neck of the woods but it wasn't green for long. I had been messing about with matches and somehow a small fire in the den we had made behind the back of our house became a large one. Suddenly the dell, where we used to spend endless days grass-sledging on pieces of cardboard, was ablaze. The situation was out of control and the fire brigade had to be rushed out to avert a disaster. It wouldn't have been so bad except my dad's new job was as a fireman and it was his colleagues who had to put out the inferno. That was Dad's turn to smack me.

Mr Stead, the headmaster at my junior school, did not miss his opportunity to administer a spanking either. A good man, but a strict disciplinarian, Mr Stead was one of those people who hummed in an animated way as he walked – 'bom-bom, bom-ba-bom' – that sort of thing. Anyway I was playing hide and seek one day and though I say so myself I had a bit of a talent for this game – I hid in a dustbin for two hours on one occasion. Most of the school's hiding places had been exhausted but I had the bright idea to sneak into Mr Stead's office and lie under his desk. It was a winner. Unfortunately a few minutes into my vigil the door creaked open and I heard the dreaded 'bom-bom, bom-ba-bom'. My blood turned to ice. I was collared. The smacked bottom for myself and my cousin Paul, whom I was playing with, came in front of the whole school next morning. Mr Stead had hands like shovels and it hurt.

All these beatings should maybe have turned me away from corporal punishment but I think it plays an important role in

16

shaping kids. I don't welcome the clampdown on the physical side which has occurred in recent years. The relaxation in discipline in schools has contributed to declining standards, something I saw at first hand during my time in the police. The world has gone mad when a teacher has to worry about being attacked while going about his work and surely a parent should not have to worry about being taken to court for telling off a child? The sad fact is the kids themselves lose out because without discipline they cannot hope to structure their lives. Our family didn't have a lot of money and we didn't live in a salubrious area but we were taught right from wrong. I had the capacity to become a tearaway but I didn't. In my case the big stick approach was essential.

My parents tried other approaches. I was often sent to my room for being naughty but invariably they would find me dangling out of the window entertaining the other kids in the street below. Saturday afternoon's shopping expedition on the bus into Dewsbury, where I was born a healthy 7lb 3oz, often turned into a running battle with Mum. Good behaviour meant I was allowed a toy and an ice cream but of course not just anything would do. I wanted the most expensive toy and largest ice cream. If I didn't get it, I would kick off. In the end the hassle became too much, she gave up and packed me off with my dad. It proved a fateful decision.

For Dad Saturdays in winter meant playing rugby union for the mighty Cleckheaton. He was a loyal club man, the type everyone needs, and played his games in the second and third teams. Dad was a back row forward who graduated to hooker towards the end of his career – he never played for the 1st XV. Not that the 1sts were anything special. Cleck have always been a junior club, never rising above the beer and fags rugby of North-East Division One. What Cleck was, and is, to me though is a reassuring place, somewhere that is always the same where I can meet friends for a beer or take the kids. It is a Sports Club which caters for bowls and cricket as well but it retains that special, very friendly atmosphere of a rugby club. I am unashamedly passionate about Cleckheaton because I love it. It stands for something. I have never forgotten Cleckheaton during the highest points of my career. I wore the club's socks for my first England trial and when I was interviewed on television after the Lions had won the 1997 series in South Africa I passed on my best to the 200 people watching at the club.

Cleckheaton's ground, Moorend, isn't the most welcoming of places with the constant hum of the M62 in the background. The fumes from the neighbouring factory which made brake linings used to make it a pretty unpleasant place to train as well. But it is home. From my earliest recollections it always was. When I was little there were very few other kids who travelled with the team but I made friends easily and more often than not managed to set up a match of my own with any opposition offspring. I had greeted the welcome home party who met us at Southampton docks when we returned from South Africa with the announcement, 'I've got a rugby ball', and Saturdays with Dad gave me the perfect opportunity to use it. Occasionally, when I was lucky, I was allowed in the bath with the team which was a fantastic treat.

I grew up in a rugby clubhouse which is really a wonderful environment, and was part of the furniture at Cleckheaton. As well as four senior teams they had a strong mini-rugby set-up and that gave me my first taste of playing matches and like all other children I loved the competition. Motivating kids on the sports field is pointless – they are naturally competitive. Life has gone full circle now and I help to coach the little

18

ones at Cleck where the eldest of my three children, Lloyd, plays. I know this is one place where I can turn my back for a minute or two and let him play without any worry about what sort of people are round the corner. It is an oasis of old-fashioned values in a world which can be full of concerns for parents.

I try to teach the juniors the importance of taking part but I can understand them just wanting to win. At their age that was all I was interested in doing. Sometimes I would take the pursuit of victory too far but when I did lose I was never one to sulk – the bitter pill would only make me more determined next time. To be honest defeat was almost unknown in those days because we had a hell of a side – the All Blacks of under-9s rugby. Yorkshire Television came down to one of our matches to do a feature on our opponents Moortown, from Leeds, who were supposed to be world beaters. We stuffed them and a tiny scrum-half named Bentley scored a couple of tries. I don't exactly know why I was scrum-half – probably because I liked to touch the ball as often as possible. My halfback partner was Simon Irving, who played for England B before turning to rugby league with Leeds and Keighley.

Trying to keep us on the straight and narrow were our coaches Joe Broomhead and Bob Butterfield, whose brother Jeff had become Cleckheaton's first British Lion on the 1955 tour to South Africa. It wasn't easy but we made all the pain worthwhile for our coaches in the end. Morley, one of Yorkshire's best sides, held an annual mini-rugby festival to which the county's finest clubs were invited. Jeff and Bob had asked if Cleckheaton could compete in it but were refused entry on the grounds that we were not strong enough. They were upset but asked again the following year and Cleck were eventually allowed in. We won the tournament. I also played some rugby at Headlands Junior School where Roger Hallas – the father of my former Halifax teammate Graeme – set up a team. The first medal I won was in a sevens event for the school.

I was never an academic but I was bright enough to go on to Heckmondwike Grammar School instead of the local secondary modern school and I eventually passed six 'O' levels, which was a job well done for me. My reports were always the same. The gist was 'likeable, well-mannered but easily distracted'. I liked French despite being hopeless at it and didn't mind maths and geography either; it was just that all the best people, those I wanted to spend time with, were into sport.

The problem with Heckmondwike though – apart from an initiation ceremony which involved being dropped on to a bed of roses – was that there was no rugby. It was a soccer school. Still, it didn't really matter, soccer was still sport. Being the noisiest I was elected soccer captain, an esteemed position which was not warranted by my skill levels. In today's game I would be a limited version of David Batty although I sometimes played more like Nora. I had to grab my rugby fix elsewhere.

It came on a Sunday morning at Cleckheaton and a Saturday afternoon at Dewsbury Moor amateur rugby league club where some of my junior school friends played. This early example of cross-code experimentation was not without its sacrifices. It was three miles to Dewsbury Moor from our house and I had to cycle there for training. In the dark. Nevertheless I enjoyed playing the game which I had heard Eddie Waring describe on *Grandstand* on a Saturday afternoon and had seen on the terraces at Headingley. Cleck did not have older youth teams so rugby league took over for a while and I played at Dewsbury Moor on and off until I was 19. In my heart I secretly still wanted to be Gareth Edwards though.

My family background was in union and the facilities were better – league clubs often played on parks and a shower consisted of a bucket of cold water on the touchline. For me the 13-man game was really just a way of filling in time when there wasn't a union team to play for at Cleck. Quite a lot of kids in the area played both: there was no segregation at this age group which made it all the more ridiculous later on. Kids have no difficulty adapting because they always play the same way. They all want the ball in their hands and nobody wants to kick – so a match of either code resembles bees buzzing around a honeypot.

A brief flirtation with the trumpet told me I would never make a musician. While others were getting into Madness or Pink Floyd I couldn't decide whether I was a mod or a punk and my hair, which has always been either short or shorter, never lent itself to heavy metal. Pop stardom was abandoned in favour of wall-to-wall sport. I kept wicket for Cleckheaton 2nd XI in the Bradford League, ran the 100 metres and 1,500 metres at school sports day and even played crown green bowls in the Spen Valley League and Mirfield League for Cleck. I couldn't help it really: Dad represented Yorkshire at it. As you would expect in this sports-mad part of the world, crown green bowls is extremely competitive and there is some good money to be won at it.

Cricket, not rugby, gave me the first of my nine or ten broken noses. I was in the nets at Cleck and top-edged a hook shot straight into my face. Bleeding like a tap, I was carted off to Batley Hospital where a doctor took one look at the injury, grabbed my broken nose and yanked it back into position. It hurt so much I made a pledge not to go to hospital when I broke my nose in future which I have kept to this day.

Doctors seem to have it in for me. When I was seven I broke my left wrist in a go-kart accident but the hospital staff only bandaged it up at first and I spent a tortuous night blubbing away at home in agony. Next day they put a pot on it but it turned out to be too tight and after lots more pain they had to take it off and have another go.

Cross-country was one of my strong points. I was favourite to win the school event one year and was waiting by the start line when my attention became distracted by the girls' race. The power of the female form held my attention to such an extent that I missed the start of our event and set off 200 yards behind the main pack. I came second.

Sport and spills left little time for girlfriends in adolescence. Alcohol too remained largely a hidden pleasure – although a few of us did develop a taste for a neighbour's sherry which he kindly left unguarded in an unlocked shed. I am grateful that these pleasures in life did not take over – I've seen too many promising players give up the chance of making it at top level by succumbing to the twin temptations. If you look after the rugby the beer and the women will look after themselves. Well, that's how it happened for me anyway!

Chapter 2

Will Carling only broke into the England team as early as he did because of his background. Twice in two seasons I had gone head to head with Carling and destroyed him.

He was playing for Durham at the time while I had just made the Yorkshire side and we were both building up reputations. Before he went off injured at Morley in November 1986 I ran through him like a knife through butter and scored a couple of tries in a 37–10 victory. That was my first season of county rugby. When our next meeting came along at Otley the following season our careers had developed to the point where it was effectively a showdown between the two of us for a place in the powerful North division backs. Divisional rugby was a turn-off for the spectators – with so much at stake in terms of England selection the matches tended to be disappointing – but as a player, once you had cracked that, the international stage beckoned. I knew what was on the line that day and I was bouncing off the walls of the dressing room before kick-off. There was only one thing on my mind – getting Carling.

There had been some confusion over where I would play on the day despite the fact that I had become established as a centre. Mike Harrison, who led England in the first World Cup, dropped out of training on Thursday night and I was asked by the Yorkshire coach John Shepherd if I would take his place on the wing. I said I would for the team's sake but I was unhappy about it and after talking to my dad about the situation I decided that for my future's sake I had to take on Carling again. I rang John back and said I would understand if he left me out but I had to play centre or nowhere. That left him a difficult choice because Bryan Barley, another England candidate, was also in the running but he plumped for me. I was determined not to let him down.

Carling was the next big thing, the talk of the changing rooms and in many ways we were similar players. We both enjoyed having the ball in our hands and running strongly with it. There was no doubt Carling was talented but the edge I had over him at that time was mental strength. In the toilets before the game Carling asked a couple of the Yorkshire lads what position I was playing and they told him that he would have to deal with me, with a certain amount of glee. He looked scared and he was right to. I tore him to shreds. The game, played out in front of a packed and passionate crowd at Otley, went perfectly for me. I scored a try, flattened Carling and produced one of my finest games. The crowd gave me a rapturous ovation. It was hard, physical rugby of the kind I love and I revelled in it.

I was still on a high the next day when the North squad assembled at Morley. The management had promised that the side for the divisional championship would be picked on form and I knew I had to be in it. As we sat in the dressing room Geoff Cooke, then the North's manager, started to read out the team: '15 – Langford, 14 – Harrison, 13 – . . .' Then he paused. I could tell something was wrong. He went on to say how centre had been the hardest position of all to choose and how well I had done but that the management wanted to give Carling another chance. What the management was doing was admitting they were making the wrong decision. It was pretty awkward for Will but for me it was devastating. I did not hear the rest of the side. I was upset and confused and as we filed out on to the pitch to do some training drills my head went completely. I told Cooke I was going for a shower and left. I did not figure in the North squad again that season.

I felt wet inside with despair. I knew – the whole team knew – it should have been me. What hurt so much was they had gone back on their word and picked Carling on reputation. I can see now looking back that it was part of Cooke's wider plan – to put him on the conveyor belt to the England captaincy – but that was little consolation at the time. I hated Carling for it.

My feelings towards him had not altered when we were picked to tour Australia and Fiji with England in 1988. By the time we reached Fiji for the last match of the tour Carling was in the side and I had been dropped. Cooke, now the England manager, organized a full-contact training session with me in the stiffs up against Carling. These are confrontational at the best of times with those frustrated at not being picked trying to show why they should have been included. The sight of Carling running at me was a red rag to a bull.

I hit him a couple of times with pretty solid tackles that conveyed what I felt. What did he do? He went up to Cooke and complained about it. I couldn't believe it – this was not schools rugby it was an international training session. Cooke came over and asked me to take it easy but I argued that it should be either contact or non-contact not something in between. He thought for a while and declared the session was now non-contact. Just to suit Will.

The first time I ever saw Cooke was after a Roses game down at Headingley. He was a very smart, articulate individual who demanded attention by his mere presence. He came over to me and congratulated me and told me how well I was doing and then walked out again. 'Great,' I thought. 'Who are you?' I hadn't a clue who he was. I asked the lads and was told he was a North selector. He was obviously the man to impress.

I met Cooke a number of times afterwards but I felt he never quite clicked with me. He always seemed to be holding part of himself back. I prefer the type of person who puts all his cards on the table but Cooke wasn't that sort with anyone. He was a cautious Cumbrian whose strength was in his evaluation of people. Not one for the limelight, he spent most of his time in the background observing. He wasn't one of the boys, certainly.

Sometimes even now I wonder how different my life would have been if Cooke had given me my just desserts with the North. But could I have been England captain instead of Carling? The answer, unfortunately, is no.

Carling made the most of his opportunities and became a great player but he was handed something on a plate I could never have had. He was sent to the right school, Sedbergh, and came from army officer stock whereas I was a sheet-metal worker's son from Cleckheaton. It wasn't Will's fault but he was born to be king while I could never have been anything but a courtier.

Rugby union has always reeked of the old boy network and I have had to put up with it all my life. I'm not a class warrior or some chip-shouldered northerner but my wife Sandy always says to me that my accent becomes stronger when I am talking to well-spoken people. She says it makes me sound rougher. I suppose that's true, but the way I talk does not make me any worse or better than the next man. I'm well-mannered and courteous and I'm proud of the fact that I am what I am and have never tried to change it.

Yet union has changed. It has been completely transformed by the arrival of professionalism. Union realized it had to embrace all-comers and dispel the cliques if it wanted to put bums on seats. The flag-bearers for professional rugby were Saracens who employed a rugby league man, Peter Deakin, to bring in cheerleaders and other innovations like motorized kicking tees. The result was a good day out which attracted all sorts of supporters who might never have looked at union in its old form. The snob factor is in retreat and has all but disappeared.

Diehards still remain. When the Paul brothers and Gary Connolly had their spells in union they were given a hard time by sections of the press. People criticized Connolly's defence at Harlequins and at first glance he didn't appear to be the player he was in league. There was a reason for that though. His union teammates were so far behind in terms of defensive organization that he was left exposed. When league and union began to mix, union was forced to see how it had to change. Union has come to respect league because it has had to.

There was never any problem between the players but the committee men in their Barbours were the ones putting up the barriers, bent on hanging on to their own private clubs. I first came across the class differences when I made the move, at 18, from Cleckheaton to Otley.

At the time Headingley, which later merged with Roundhay

to form Leeds, was probably the strongest club in Yorkshire. They were also the most snobby. They had approached me to play for them but they forgot to phone me to arrange to train with them so I agreed to go to homely Cross Green instead. I liked the people down at Otley. They seemed to care more.

Otley weren't a bad side – they were probably ranked in a group with Halifax, Sheffield and Roundhay, behind Headingley and Wakefield in the Yorkshire pecking order. Moving to Otley was a stepping stone to county rugby, which still ruled the roost then and was a massive leap in standard for me. I had been to the club after a colts match between Cleckheaton and Otley for a big game and was impressed by their set-up and the number of supporters they had. They were all amateurs but they trained hard and I thought I would fit in well.

Otley didn't have the biggest set of forwards but there was a good set of backs including James Dracup, a very talented footballer who came out of retirement to partner me in the centre. We were chalk and cheese – he was a toff and a half but we got on very well and he was good for my game, bringing me on no end. Otley allowed me to play as I wanted, there were no restrictive game plans, and although it was trial and error on occasions I learned a hell of a lot. In every respect.

Part of the arrangement which took me to Otley was the promise of the first car I could call my own. I was worried at the time because this amounted to professionalism and I thought I would be in big trouble if anyone found out. Peter Winterbottom, who played for Headingley at the time, knew the woman who the club had bought it off and accused me of accepting the car from Otley. I had to lie to him and deny it. In hindsight the car, a white Ford Escort Mark II, was the most ridiculous example of shamateurism imaginable. It was

a complete wreck. The petrol gauge was broken, always showing three-quarters full so I regularly ran out of fuel. Worse, I
was driving along with Simon Irving one night having had too
much to drink when the gearstick came off in my hand. That's
all you need when you're trying to look inconspicuous.

Soon after I'd joined, the club's scrum-half, Mark
Waddington, invited me to his birthday party to make me feel
welcome. He told me I should wear black tie and that Sandy,
who was my girlfriend then, should come in a nice dress. After
fathoming out what black tie was I managed to get hold of a
suit and we duly arrived. Much to Sandy's horror, the short
frock she had put on did not quite coincide with what the rest
of the women were wearing. They were all done out in ballgo-
wns and Sandy felt like a waitress. The players never once
looked down their noses though and everyone was lovely and
welcoming. It was just a social scene we had not experienced
before. I was happy in my new surroundings and although I
still managed the odd game of rugby league at Dewsbury
Moor (under false names) union had got me.

We had a good fixture list and I made my debut against
Jedforest. The next week we played Gosforth, who were a
superb side with David Johnson at fly-half and Chalky White
at prop. In those days there would be a series of games in
Yorkshire each weekend and the county's rugby followers
would go to the best one. This particular day it was our
match. Roared on by a big crowd we beat Gosforth 14–13
with the help of a Japanese referee; the *Yorkshire Post*
reported on Monday morning that Otley had found a new
rising son. I was on top of the world – but I was soon brought
down to earth.

Full of my own importance I went to watch Yorkshire beat

Lancashire in a midweek game at Orrell. I knew Otley were due to play Wakefield at the weekend so I approached Mike Harrison, the future England captain who had just been playing for Yorkshire, in the bar afterwards. I mouthed off that although he didn't know who I was at the moment, he would do next week. Mike's a pretty laid-back, calm sort of bloke and looked suitably bemused. Anyway Otley went to College Grove and were duly thrashed 49–3 with Harrison scoring a superb length-of-the-field try after Steve Townend had kicked the ball to him across his own 22. I had been used to making five or six breaks per game but coming up against a drift defence for the first time I didn't get a look in. The learning curve had begun.

Next up was an away trip to Kelso and my first appointment with a young tearaway by the name of Alan Tait, who had already played for Scotland. They had another international, Roger Baird, on the wing. He got a bashing from me but unfortunately we lost 31–15. I was approached in the toilets after that game by a scout representing Hunslet. I had already been given a bloke's card at Wakefield but I really had no interest in turning codes at that stage. I was chasing my England rainbow.

To be honest, I looked down my nose at professional rugby league at that stage. All the approaches I was receiving seemed so shady that it did not hold much appeal. Because of the barriers between the two codes they were all made on the sly with promises of inducements if I went, but I didn't feel I could trust them. Even later on in my career I had to be careful. Halifax wanted me to sign a new contract with them on the pitch at half-time in front of their supporters, which I almost did until I realized they had altered it without me knowing. I put pen to paper in front of thousands of witnesses but none of them knew I had actually moved the contract and signed a blank envelope instead.

The first time I began to take notice of the league interest was when Leeds coach Maurice Bamford came to watch me play in the Yorkshire Cup final at the end of the 1986–7 season. This was a marvellous date in the rugby calendar with the oldest cup in rugby, T'Owd Tin Pot, up for grabs. It brought everyone out of the woodwork. We were up against Morley in the final at their place but even though we had the bigger pack we contrived to lose, because we ran everything. I tried too hard, took all the wrong options and had a nightmare. The call from Maurice never came.

The defeat was all the more galling after the way we'd pulled off our semi-final victory over favourites Wakefield. It was my penalty in the last five minutes which won the tie at a sodden Cross Green. It was 30 metres out near the touchline, and I picked out the only dry part of the pitch to take it from. I was a very erratic goalkicker and from the moment I struck it this one never looked like making it, but somehow the ball limped over and put us in the final. That Yorkshire Cup final display was the second worst of my career. The absolute rock bottom did not receive as much coverage.

That was when I played for the West Yorkshire Police. I had broken my nose playing for Otley on the Saturday and I turned up on the Tuesday for West Yorkshire's cup semi-final against Northumbria at Sandal with the carrot of a place in the British Police side dangling in front of me. I was persuaded to play and everything that could have gone wrong, did. If I could have been substituted I would have been but the game went into its final minute with me still on the field and us just behind. We were awarded a simple penalty in front of the posts to win a place in the final. But inexplicably I picked up the ball, tapped it to myself and blew the chance.

I had been under some pressure to play for the force since I was turning out for the football team as a midfield cruncher but not bothering with the rugby. Why? Well, there is nothing more brutal than police sport – it is barbaric. Being sorted out by some thug was not my idea of fun when I was trying to carve out a career at club level. I did play often enough eventually to make the British Police side for a game against the full Lancashire line-up. Inevitably that descended into one big scrap with me trading blows with Nigel Heslop, another copper who later went on to play for England. It was such a ferocious dust-up we refused to shake hands afterwards. Always a tell-tale sign.

A more varied rugby education was taking place at Otley. Off the field as well as on it. The club went on a three-week tour to Florida which, as you might guess, was not solely about rugby. We often ended up in a bar called Hooters where the waitresses wore little and we drank lots. Pitchers full of lager were the order of the day and I used to make my way through the crowds to the bar, get served but be hijacked on the way back by thirsty and lazy teammates and have to give it all away. The worst culprit was the captain Dave Garforth, so having fought my way to the bar yet again I decided on revenge. I ordered a half-full pitcher of lager and topped it up by relieving myself at the bar. I walked past Dave who duly demanded a glass of 'lager' which he downed in one. I gave him a few more for good measure. Under Florida law I was too young to drive but this did not stop me having a go behind the wheel of our mini-bus.

We were backed up at a set of traffic lights behind four convertibles so I thought we would have a bit of fun. I gently nudged into the back of the first one and squeezed it forward into the next car. Then I kept going. Each car was nudged forward into the back of the one in front until the foremost one was pushed through the red light. There were horns blaring, tyres screeching and a lot of rugby players laughing.

Otley had spotted me as a Cleckheaton colt where I had made my mark after a difficult start. I was still a scrum-half in my formative colts years and had found life as a 16-year-old against 19-year-olds a scary experience. I managed to get rid of two fly-halves in one game against Rotherham by throwing them hospital passes when I was in danger of being hit. My teammates used to take their revenge by stripping me and sending me off home through the streets of Cleckheaton naked. Character building I think they called it.

As well as being a bridge between mini and senior rugby, the whole experience took us from being schoolboys to the adult world. There was a marvellous camaraderie which involved 30 of us going to the pub together. The older ones looked after the youngsters with no money by buying them drinks. We had a lot of fun and played some decent rugby.

My move to centre came after a terrible first-half performance from Cleck colts in a cup match at Goole which persuaded the coach John Barraclough to swap me and the centre Andy Heptinstall over for the second half. The side was transformed and I never played scrum-half again. As I got older I did, however, make a brief and surprisingly successful one-off appearance as the smallest No. 8 in Yorkshire colts history in a regional trial at Ionians. Simon Irving and I had graduated into Cleckheaton 1st XV by then so after being selected for the final trial we raced down to the club only to find the game against Bradford Salem had already started.

Cleck had only 13 men on the field so we changed in a split second, raced on and in perfect Roy of the Rovers style I made a break and gave the try-scoring pass to my teammate Andy Foster which won the game 9–8.

Simon was a centre by now as well and we made an effective partnership because we were both physical players – rugby league types, I suppose. He liked to hit opponents hard around the legs while I scragged them around the head. We backed each other up and had the sort of relationship that would normally be associated with the front row.

The final Yorkshire colts trial was at Cleckheaton in 1984 which was great for me and Simon and we did enough to be selected together. To wear a Yorkshire shirt at whatever level is an extremely proud moment. It can be difficult to explain to people from other parts of the country where county allegiance is not so strong but for me the feeling was an emotional one. County rugby was the springboard for everything I achieved in either code.

Swelled with pride we used to go out after games in our county blazers thinking we looked the bees' knees. Actually we looked like we needed a good hiding. After one game our back row of Rod Hogg, John Dudley and Clive Williams plus Simon and myself ended up in a nightclub called Panache in Mirfield. We were carrying on alarmingly and I ended up so drunk I fell off a high stool and was unable to raise myself from the floor. I was 'helped' out of the club.

Thanks to the shrewd guidance of Alan Roche, who was in charge of Yorkshire, I progressed through the North colts and on to the final England colts trial at Birmingham where a mini-bus from Cleck deposited planted spectators around the field. Their instructions were to mutter 'that Bentley looks a good prospect' in a variety of regional accents and it must have worked a treat as I was picked for England on the wing after being shunted out there for part of the trial. I could not care less – I would have played prop for my country. The ones whose names were read out were asked to stay, the rest had to leave. It was all very regimental. Strangely very few of that side went on to make their mark in the higher levels of rugby.

The northern contingent had one or two preconceived ideas about our southern counterparts. A lot of us had played some rugby league and we thought we were harder than the soft lads from the south but the internationals against Wales, Italy and France brought us all together. We became quite a close side. One of the most important turning points of my career came on England colts' 1985 summer tour to Canada. From being an average player who made up the numbers I could feel myself blossoming into something better. I was bigger, faster and suddenly I was tearing up defences. The tour went superbly, I was top try-scorer, we won the Test and I returned full of confidence. Yet it could all have been so different.

We were serving a beer ban in the early stages of the trip which wouldn't have been a problem except my 19th birthday coincided with it. Sixty people down at Cleck had donated £5 each to help pay my way so I had money to burn and a few of us sneaked out for a celebratory pint. We returned in a terrible state of disrepair several hours later and I had to be carried back into the place where we were staying. I collapsed on the floor and was dragged by my teammates feet first up the stairs with my head bumping against each one. Put to bed by my thoughtful colleagues, I thought I was having a nightmare when I was prodded awake by the team manager Mike Glogg who had heard the commotion. He told me as a punishment I would be duty boy the next day which meant organizing the kit and doing all the menial tasks no-one liked to bother with. I was also ordered to his office where, still half-cut, I was informed that he was considering sending me home because of my behaviour. Sobriety hit me in an instant. I don't know whether he was bluffing but I really knuckled down after that and when he wrote his report to Yorkshire after the tour he said I had been exemplary. There was no mention of my birthday party.

The trip was the highlight of my season. Except, of course, the Cleckheaton versus Old Brodleians Boxing Day match. I had grown up watching this annual ritual where the excesses of the previous day were barely worked off before they were added to in the clubhouse afterwards. The away games at Brods were often played in shocking conditions perched, as it is, on the tops above Halifax. This time the game was at home but the pitch was extremely icy and had to survive an inspection. The match went ahead and we lost as usual but I was at last part of the tradition, playing in front of the club's biggest crowd of the year. Even when I turned out for Leeds or Halifax rugby league clubs in later years I would return to Cleck in the afternoon for the knees-up. It was always a fantastic occasion.

One season a shoulder injury kept me out of Otley's Boxing Day match against Headingley so inevitably I found my way over to Cleck for the party. The situation went rapidly out of control after I downed a pint of vodka in one and I ended up crawling about on the bedroom floor of my cousin Steve's house in serious trouble. Simon Irving, who always seemed to be about for these sorts of carry-ons, heard me throwing up on a brand-new carpet and wrenched open the bedroom door to witness this pathetic sight, only to crack it against my swirling head. I was poured into a taxi and left in a crumpled heap on my mum and dad's doorstep – what a lovely Christmas present for them.

My one regret was only playing 17 games for Cleckheaton that season before I left. You needed to play 20 to be awarded a 1st XV tie. The club presented me with a Cleck shirt at a celebratory dinner after I returned from the Lions tour but there was no tie with it. I didn't expect one and I wouldn't have accepted it. That honour has to be earned. Who knows, maybe I will earn the right to wear it one day.

Eggbox, as Simon Irving is also known, also played a part in my meeting Sandy. I had enjoyed a few tentative meetings with girls but nothing which would justify being called a relationship. In fact I was quite naive. Simon and I had been having several quiet beers at The Grey Ox, an out-of-the-way pub in nearby Hartshead. We had noticed a couple of girls in the bar about our age but we had brown liquid on our minds and hadn't paid much attention to them and at kicking-out time we left to try to flag down a taxi outside. I rolled up my trouser leg and started wafting it around in front of car headlights to get us a lift and when one slowed down at the junction Eggbox took his chance and opened the door. Inside were the two girls from the pub. We invited ourselves round for coffee thinking our luck might be in, a notion which was rudely shattered when we arrived at one of their houses to find her family standing there. One awkward cuppa later we disappeared.

A couple of weeks later we were in Cleckheaton when we heard a horn honk and turned around to find our host from that night had pulled up. This time her passenger had changed and I was introduced to Sandy. They offered us another lift and I remember thinking Sandy, who was a local hairdresser, looked a good catch. Nothing would probably have come of it but for me rejecting an offer from Eggbox to go to a stag do in Bradford some time afterwards and wandering into a pub called Foxy's in Cleckheaton on my own. In there was Sandy. She came over, we chatted and as I was in my dad's car I took her back to her house for a coffee. As I was leaving I plucked up the courage to kiss her goodnight. I leaned forward to press my lips against her cheek but somehow she managed to drop her doorkey and in that split second bent down to pick it up. I ended up kissing her on the top of the head and cursing all the way home. She must have liked my style though as she ended up going out with me and hasn't managed to escape yet.

The move across the Pennines from Otley to Sale in the summer of 1987 came at the right time for me, broadening my horizons as a rugby player. Sale is a strong rugby area and it has always managed to attract quality players. The presence of Fran Cotton and Steve Smith helped in this respect. They built a leisurewear empire, Cotton Traders, together and made a great double act. I always got on well with Fran. He thrives on controversy and isn't scared of speaking his mind – he should be a Yorkshireman really.

I had established myself in the Yorkshire side and had scored a couple of tries in the 1986–7 county championship semi-final against North Midlands, a game we won 24–0. Watching the game was Fran who was spying for Sale. It is a good job he did not pick the final to judge me on because I was punched off the ball early on and played the rest of the match against Middlesex in a daze. I hazily remember that we won Yorkshire's first county championship since 1953 with Rob Andrew and Rory Underwood on our side.

Sale were keen and did everything the right way, talking to Otley first, and with other Yorkshiremen like Simon Tipping and Martin Whitcombe already travelling across to play for the club, I signed on for the 1987–8 season. I felt it was the correct decision, although the extra travelling that their top-rate fixtures demanded gave the three of us the chance to get into some scrapes together.

We caused a bit of a scene one night at a hotel which was foolishly holding a wedding reception as well as hosting us. We added ourselves to the guest-list and, while no-one was looking, half-inched the top tier of the cake. The trail of crumbs led straight to our room so the hotel management retrieved it before too much had been eaten.

The train journey to an away tie at London Irish in the cup that season turned into a drinking contest between myself, Tipping and an attractive young girl sat opposite who turned out to be one of that rare breed – a model with a taste for McEwan's Export. Tipping and I downed 12 cans each in the three hours it took to reach King's Cross from Leeds and the girl bought us one at the station just to top us up. By the time we reached the team hotel Tipping and I were steaming, which was unheard of for me because I was usually disciplined the night before a game, even in these amateur days.

We were reimbursed with our travel expenses – but not for our drinking spree – while we sat in the hotel bar. For some reason I was given a little bit more than Tipping. I said I would sort it out later with him but he demanded his share there and then. It was only a matter of a pound or two so I didn't see the urgency. But suddenly I found myself on my back, pinned to the ground by my neck looking up at Tipping's fist. Fortunately a couple of our teammates intervened or I think he would have killed me. I know Yorkshiremen are supposed to be tight but this was ridiculous.

We used to be given our expenses in brown envelopes which looked a lot dodgier than it was. I used to 'earn' about £40 for each trip across to Sale to play or train which was beer money really. Other clubs in the south with rich patrons used to be far more generous, although, like them, Sale were well connected enough to offer jobs to players who needed them.

Sale was another step up in terms of quality of players and surroundings. I was earmarked to fill the boots of Tony Bond who had moved to Askeans but I didn't feel any pressure because I was confident of delivering the goods. Part of my preparation each week was to look at the big-name players who I was coming up against because mixing it with them inspired me. I didn't feel out of my depth even though the defences I was running into were better.

Our forwards did not win all that much ball – as with all the clubs I have played with except Newcastle – but we had one backs move which I used to call at regular intervals, entitled 'give it to me and I'll have a go'. It was none too sophisticated but it emphasised my desire to get my hands on the ball at all times, an instinct I have always had to work hard to dilute. I had a love-hate relationship with my centre partner Phil Stansfield who always wanted a piece of the action too. In one game against Wasps we both went for the same ball, bungled things and ended up fighting with each other on the opposition line.

Eggbox had moved on to Headingley by the time I went to Sale which meant a mouthwatering personal confrontation when the two clubs met. There was pride at stake. I scooted round him twice in quick succession and laughed at him as I went past which I knew he would appreciate. Later, when I went to retrieve a chip over my head, Eggbox came charging in and punched me on the back of the head before starting to giggle. It was all playful stuff but Stansfield did not see it the same way and came wading in to have a pot at Eggbox. I had to plead with him not to flatten my friend.

To be honest I enjoyed trading punches. There had been a memorable melee against West Hartlepool with Otley when all four centres including me were going at it hammer and tongs while the forwards looked on in admiration. However I had to be careful because I had been warned by those closest to me not to pick up the reputation of being a dirty player. Besides, being smacked hurt. We had a second row called John Howe who was an immense bloke and looked as nasty as you get on a rugby field. On one occasion he was so pleased to see me he beat me up. I've never taken a hiding like it – punches, knees, kicks – you name it. It never seemed to stop. Whitcombe and Tipping looked on laughing at John's own particular way of saying hello. Quite a character, John sadly died on 30 March 1992 on a rugby field at Morley after suffering a heart attack.

Chapter 3

My season at Sale saw a league system introduced for rugby union in England. It wasn't a conspicuous success for us – we came bottom – but it was the start of a structure for the game in England which brought great rewards. From being embarrassing underachievers at international level, England finally began to punch their weight. The presence of a competitive structure rather than the age-old friendlies must have played a major part in the transformation. It sharpened everyone up: clubs that dragged their feet would face relegation and tangible prizes were there for those who fought their way to the top. There was no comfort zone any more.

Although it is hard to imagine life without leagues now, it took some time for their importance to be recognized. I chose to play for Yorkshire ahead of Sale during the county championship and it was through that competition that I made my way into the England final trial at Twickenham. I got there despite not making the North side. The England trial took place on an awful day but I ran around Rory Underwood for the only try and earned a place in the England B team to shadow the full side in France. I was chuffed – from there I could strike for a place in the full team.

The B international was played in the Jean Bouin Stadium, just behind the Parc-des-Princes, on the morning of the Five Nations game. It was a tough baptism for me. The Bayonne Express, Patrick Lagisquet, had been dropped by France and I was given the job of marking him. I did OK but one of my main concerns was keeping my England shirt from the game. The tradition was to exchange with your opponent and I brought along an Otley one to swap on the off-chance that Lagisquet wasn't paying full attention. However he was great and when we shook hands he gave me his shirt but insisted I keep my own which was a wonderful gesture. It was one that Rory made sure was repeated on my full England debut for which I will always be grateful.

Alan Davies and Dave Robinson were in charge of that England B side, which was a mixture of young hopefuls and a couple of experienced players like Gary Pearce and Steve Bainbridge. They had done a good job bonding us together into a side because obviously we each had our own ambitions. They made sure there was no friction and we played for the team. Within that framework I managed to score a hat trick against Spain at Imber Court and also played reasonably well against Italy at Leicester. We had some useful turns: Ollie Redman and Andy Robinson, for instance.

It wasn't like the full international set-up. We used to turn up the day before games and the hotels weren't quite what the top boys would be given but we didn't mind – we weren't in them for long. In B international rugby, it was just accepted that we could go out and paint the town red after games. There was no question of the management turning a blind eye – they were invariably with us. As long as we didn't smash up hotel rooms or get ourselves into serious trouble, it was OK.

We celebrated in traditional style in Paris after the game against France, starting early on the beer, and were buzzing by the time of the main game. Unfortunately there had been a cock-up over our ticket allocation and so the England B squad ended up climbing over the walls in our blazers and ties to get in for the game. An England side featuring a young debutant at centre called Will Carling lost 10–9 and we met up with them afterwards.

Will fitted into the common-sense gang with Rob Andrew, Simon Halliday, Jonathan Webb et al. but for some reason I seemed to gravitate towards the mad forwards like Wade Dooley. For some reason Wade and I had never got along – I don't know why but I had the feeling he had it in for me. It was probably me being a gobby young upstart whereas Wade had been around the circuit for a while. Anyway he wasn't keen. I was full of beer and Pernod and decided to have it out with the Blackpool Tower. He wasn't in the best of moods after the loss and the dispute escalated to the point where we ended up buying pints of lager and pouring them over each other. With each successive pint the atmosphere grew more tense. I had just returned from the bar with a third pint destined for Dooley's colossal 6-ft 8-in frame when he clenched his fist and warned me I was history if it went over him. He was serious. Peter Winterbottom and Paul Rendall stepped in to try to calm things down and a journalist became involved before Dooley decided he wanted a quiet word with me in another bar. He wasn't taking no for an answer so I went along, expecting the worst. However we decided to drink a pint rather than throw it, smoothed things over and ever since then have got along fine.

That England B team contained three of us who were to switch to league before returning to union when it went open. The glory of playing for your country was all very well but for some there were mouths to feed back home and league was promising big money. Fly-half Peter Williams went to Salford and winger Mark Preston to Wigan soon afterwards. My move would have to wait. I had an ambition to fulfil and it wasn't long in coming.

My full international debut arrived in Dublin in April 1988. For some reason, Ireland had decided they wanted to hold a one-off Millennium Test against England at the end of the Five Nations Championship. There's nobody like the Irish for starting the celebrations early. I had been named in the squad, but with England having beaten Ireland 35–3 a matter of weeks earlier, I did not expect to play. However an injury to Mike Harrison provided me with an unexpected opportunity. I was aware he was struggling and as we trained on the Twickenham pitch I was watching every move of his to see if he would miss out. Geoff Cooke went over to him, checked him out and 20 seconds later he was heading towards me. 'Bentos, you're in,' he said.

I experienced a great surge of emotion as all the players came and congratulated me individually. I just wanted training to be over so I could tell everyone. As soon as it finished I rang my parents – they were so pleased and proud and my dad arranged to come out to Dublin to watch with his Cleck mate Donald Ross. I was on a high and just couldn't come down. There was some anxiety – would I make a mistake in front of all those people? and so on – but I tried to dispel all that.

We flew over to Dublin and had a light run-out on the

Friday before the trip to Lansdowne Road. It was the first time I had been there. Again, I visualized the game going on around me in these surroundings which was as exciting as it was nerve-wracking. Before the match I must have played it through in my mind a hundred times which is an exhausting business in itself. The tension built and built in the hours leading up to the game. I roomed with Jonathan Webb, a qualified surgeon whose access to sleeping pills could have come in handy. That night I might as well have not gone to bed for the amount of sleep I had.

There was a full house at the ground the next day, ready to roar on Ireland's every move. I took one look at the size of their forwards and decided that was one area I certainly did not want to be heading for – they looked immense. I needn't have worried. After we kicked off I didn't touch the ball for 20 minutes. I was playing outside a midfield of Rob Andrew, Will Carling and Simon Halliday and they were just set on kicking for position. When the ball eventually arrived it was a bit of a shock and I got rid of it as soon as I could. The game was much faster than what I had been used to. I had very little time on the ball and was closed down very quickly by my opposite number Michael Kiernan. We won the game 21–10, which was not a bad effort for England in those days, but I contributed virtually nothing as it flashed by before my eyes. When it ended I couldn't believe it was over so quickly. It was like an out-of-body experience – I was there and yet I wasn't there.

I remember more about being lured into a nightclub called Strings by a very attractive blonde lady in a red PVC dress following the traditional after-match dinner. I was with Andy Robinson and Paul Rendall doing damage to a considerable amount of bucks fizz. We stumbled out in the early hours to try to flag down a taxi and ended up in the fastest one imaginable – and it was free. The car was a Ford Cosworth driven by the security men who were with the team and it screeched up and whisked me and John Buckton off to the castle where we were staying. I was a policeman at the time and therefore a potential terrorist target. It would have taken a pretty bad gunman to miss me in the condition I was in. We arrived back to finding Rendall turning the top of a grand piano into a sea of Guinness. It was our job to try to finish them all. I met Steve Smith at the airport the next day and was in such an appalling state I had to refuse a drink from him. Not my usual style.

I obviously made an impression on the selectors in the bar because I was chosen for the tour to Australia and Fiji later that year. It did not do much for my rugby but the boy who flew out came back a man as a result of our off-field capers.

Looking back everything about the set-up was so amateur. The game was a hobby and a sideline for the players even though they were representing their country. We had a warm-up of sorts before matches but no warm-down afterwards, something which every club side does now to prevent stiffness. There weren't any energy drinks to replenish lost fluids – just water – in fact there was hardly any attention given to diet. Players could basically eat what they wanted when they wanted. Training consisted of long, laborious sessions with the backs practising a handful of moves rather than the short, sharp work which is preferred today. To concentrate for two and a half hours at a time was difficult – especially for me. We had to wear horrible, shiny purple tracksuits that were all the rage in 1970 and there were no weights sessions at all. As for psychologists and masseurs, they hadn't been invented as far as England were concerned. And not just England – that's how international rugby was then.

I played in the first Test at Brisbane and scored an 80-metre interception try. We lost 22–16 though and I was taught a footballing lesson on the right wing by David Campese who was on majestic form. He did not score but that had nothing to do with me. He was at the top of his game then, a very charismatic character who talked as good a match as he played. But his way of psyching me out was to not pay me any attention at all. Campese was involved all over the place as they threw everything at us. What a footballer.

He was able to pick great lines to run along and hit the ball at pace. He wasn't a robotic player – he would move to another line if he saw the space opening up – and he benefited greatly from having Michael Lynagh as his distributor. Michael used to pass the ball into mid-air and Campo would simply decide where he wanted to collect it to cause the most problems. He gave us a torrid time. I was only too aware of how well he was going but even though I appreciated his sublime talent I knew I had to do something to try and stop him. In desperation I tried to rough him up but he was pretty handy at dishing out a portion too.

Things had not gone that well for me and as the Second Test approached Cooke told me I needed a big game to make the side. I was picked for the midweek game leading up to it against New South Wales Country and there was a lot of rain before the match. I went out and bought some longer studs to compensate but they did no good at all. At one point I tripped over myself because they dug in too early which summed up a poor game on my part.

The writing was on the wall so I wasn't that upset when I missed out on selection for the Second Test. I wasn't playing well enough to merit it and had only myself to blame. So I concentrated my efforts elsewhere. During our time off we used to hang out in a pub called The Ship Inn in Brisbane. I ended up in Mick Skinner's gang – he had gone off tour after falling out with forwards coach Dave Robinson and had become a disruptive influence.

One night several of the tour party were chatting to a couple of local girls at The Ship. As always one was considerably prettier than the other. The English tourists, being gentlemen, offered to buy them both a drink. The rougher of the two said she wanted a gin and tonic and since I and Kevin Murphy, the physiotherapist, were at the bar we were told to get them. Using the technique I had picked up in Florida, I unzipped my flies and relieved myself into a glass then added a couple of ice cubes to cool things off. We handed the drinks over and watched intently as the poor girl put her glass to her lips. 'Ugh,' she cried. 'What's up?' I asked innocently. 'I ordered gin and tonic,' she said. 'Not vodka and lemonade.' One of the team, who shall remain nameless, ended up in a room kissing her – and he knew what she had been drinking.

When the time came to leave for Fiji, I almost missed the flight. A particularly heavy night had ended up with me in the wrong bedroom along with a friend from Huddersfield, Mike Lumley. A hotel search was ordered to try to track me down as the minutes ticked down to our departure and there was still no sign. Eventually Geoff Cooke, the coach, and Rory Underwood found the room and opened the door to find me sound asleep, entangled with Mike in a double bed, both completely naked. I don't think Rory approved. The highest try-scorer in English history, the highest cap-winner, but not one of the sport's most charismatic personalities. A big night out for Rory was a glass of coke and endless bars of chocolate. As for Cooke, he kept turning up like a bad penny.

After the Test in Fiji when I once again missed out I stole the match ball as a momento to take home. There was a big inquiry with Cooke demanding the culprit step forward. The investigation had snowballed to such an extent that I couldn't possibly have owned up so I sneaked it into my bag and we headed home. After an endless sequence of flights which took the best part of 48 hours I stepped off the plane at Leeds/Bradford Airport to be greeted amongst others by my little nephew Thomas. I had the perfect present for him. I unzipped the bag and fished out the stolen ball. Just as Geoff Cooke walked past.

The tone of the tour had been set by an 'acclimatization' week which had culminated in a spectacular court session. My punishment for various misdemeanours was being tied to a tree for hours, forced to drink cocktails and sing Manhattan Transfer songs. The England captain on that tour, John Orwin, added a unique personal touch by urinating all over me. Disgusting I know but I had it coming to me as I had tried the same trick on Gary Hartley, the Nottingham centre, at an England B training session. The difference was that that was down the back of his legs during a boring briefing from our coach Alan Davies. Hartley was none too impressed and gave me some impromptu sprint training.

Australia was a wonderful place to tour, particularly Brisbane which had a great way of life. Everything revolved around the beach, the drink and the women. At first glance I didn't really like Sydney – it was cold and wet when we were there – but having been back many times since it has become my favourite city. It is a real 24-hour place – just my bag. Fiji was a disappointment. Rather than the paradise island I expected, it was a dump. There was a lot of poverty and there was always a menacing air around. I was glad to leave.

In all we spent six weeks away and we bonded fantastically. It being an amateur tour there wasn't much pressure to measure up off the field, even though it was England. Fortunately there were no tabloid newshounds around in those days – they would have drowned in the amount of dirt to be found. The down side was that although we had our flights and hotels paid for we had to stump up for our own beer and phone calls home. Taking into account the unpaid leave I had to take from the police to go on the trip it cost me quite a lot of money but I wouldn't have missed it for the world.

With things starting to happen on the international front it was quite a surprise to some people when I switched codes. A shake-up in my personal life was the catalyst for a fresh start. I had treated Sandy shabbily for a while. I used to pack her in on the Friday, go out and have a great time with the lads over the weekend, then get back together with her on the Sunday. I took it for granted that she would have me back. Sandy and I had become engaged during the Hong Kong Sevens in March 1988. I had gone out there to play for The Penguins who were an invitational side cobbled together from across the world. I was the only Englishman in a squad which included three All Blacks – David Kirk, Craig Green and Wayne Smith, two Australians – Bill Calcraft and Ross Reynolds, two Welsh lads – David Pickering and Paul Turner, and one Scotsman – Rob Wainwright. We were all good rugby players but we could all drink a bit as well – except Rob, who didn't bother with that kind of thing. I spent a lot of time with the Irish Wolfhounds who were also taking part. They had such reprobates as Dave Irwin, Stuart Barnes and Barry Evans in the side. Hong Kong is one long party.

The place comes to a standstill as people from all over the world fly in to take part in a competition played in the true spirit of rugby. It is fantastic to be part of it. Some sides approach it very seriously, like the Fijians and the New Zealanders, then there are others like Australia who are able to have a good crack and perform well. Then there are teams like us who had a good crack but weren't able to perform. I was barely able to run.

The tournament was spread over the Saturday and Sunday but for some reason we turned up on the Tuesday. We had a couple of training sessions to familiarize ourselves with each other but the rest was just fun and games. We spent a lot of our time in The Bull and Bear which was home to lots of ex-pats and stayed open late enough for our requirements. Incredibly we reached the semi-finals, having knocked out France, but found a New Zealand side featuring the likes of John Kirwan and Zinzan Brooke too hot to handle.

I must have had a good tour because I telephoned Sandy in a tired and emotional state from Hong Kong to pop the question and brought her home a beautiful Cartier watch as a token of my commitment. Unfortunately it was a £7.50 fake and conked out two weeks after I gave it to her, which summed up our situation really. Five months later I broke the engagement off and although she pleaded with me to come back I refused. I went out and lived the life of Reilly. It was like being on tour again, only in Cleckheaton.

Then I heard she had started to see someone else. Suddenly I was all mixed up – this was my Sandy and I wanted her back. Of course all I had to do was turn up on her doorstep and everything would be OK again. Except it wasn't. She would not have anything to do with me and I went off the rails.

I was injured at the time and not playing any rugby and I began to drink heavily. Not only that, I ended up in a street-fight one Saturday night with a friend which ended with me headbutting him and knocking him out. I still have the scar. He was in a mess and his mother wanted him to report me to my employers, which would have been a disaster as I was still with the police at the time. He didn't because we were still mates but afterwards people close to me told me to take a good look at myself in the mirror. I had thrown Sandy away and it began to sink in that I was in danger of throwing the rest of my life away too.

I buckled down, stopped drinking and began to train hard again. I started seeing another girl and maybe this had a certain impact on Sandy because she finally agreed to take me back. I was on course again. We had only been apart for three months but it had felt like a lifetime. She was back alongside me for my next big step into the other world of rugby league.

Chapter 4

I turned down the chance to become a part of the most successful rugby club in England.

Hindsight is a wonderful gift but even with the benefit of it I know I made the right decision in rejecting Wigan. I had been receiving offers for some time when I met Maurice Lindsay, who was then the Wigan chairman, at a motorway service station. He told me he would top any bid I received from elsewhere. It was a tempting offer, sat as I was in Maurice's Mercedes, but having thought about it I decided to say no.

I had already talked to the other big-hitters in rugby league. Doug Laughton from Widnes had approached Fran Cotton after a Sale match against Broughton Park and asked for permission to talk to me. Fran, who had been the target of a few offers himself during his career and had actually agreed to join St Helens before changing his mind, had no objection. He could understand players wanting to do the best they could for themselves. Fran had done himself. He wasn't even supposed to be involved in union because he had been banned for writing a book and taking the profits. He was supposed to be out in the wilderness and the double standards that existed in rugby union then meant that officially there was no way back for him.

Geoff Cooke and Dave Robinson invited him along for one North training session at Fylde to help out with the forwards. Because of his ban Fran turned up in disguise – or so he thought. There was this giant of a man huddled inside a flimsy kagool with the hood tied around his head. The only problem was this massive chin sticking out from it. Only a complete idiot wouldn't have recognized him.

Thanks to Fran, Doug Laughton met me in one of Sale's houses near their ground at Heywood Road. He wasn't pushy – quite laid-back in fact – and when I explained to him my England ambition in union was top of my list he seemed quite understanding. In fact he was more interested in my assessment of Brimah Kebbie, whom I had played against that day and whom Doug later brought across to league.

It was only when Hull Kingston Rovers offered me £90,000 up front to join them in November 1988 that I finally decided I was going to switch codes. The experience with Sandy had shaken me up and convinced me that it was time for a new challenge. Even though everything about my background and my social life was related to rugby union, I had always been attracted to league as a game. It was quicker than union and I was curious to see how I would fit in. The only way to find out was to try.

Hull KR wanted a big-name signing to play centre and I was confident I could fulfil the job description. In reality I wanted to join Leeds. Being used to the smaller crowds of club rugby union the stage that Headingley could provide and the passion and atmosphere generated on the terraces appealed to me. I had stood there myself and watched – Leeds was the team that I had supported even though Dewsbury was my local club. In many ways Leeds were the Manchester United of rugby league. They were the glamour club and if they were interested there was only one team I wanted to join. So when a journalist rang to ask me if there was any truth in the story that I was to join Hull KR I told him I was about to sign for a rugby league club at the weekend.

This worked out perfectly as Alan Agar from Leeds heard about the story and rang me up to ask if I would be interested in joining them. I was and, having rejected Wigan's overtures, we met in The Swan pub in the city to discuss a move to Leeds. I was warned against it by John Atkinson, a Leeds legend and another policeman in the city, who thought I would struggle to break into an all international back division. However I have never been short of confidence in my ability and I was not to be put off.

I was just recovering from injury at the time and my come-back match was for West Yorkshire Police at Morley. Malcolm Reilly, the Leeds coach, came along to watch. It was the perfect chance for me to run in a couple of easy tries. He was impressed and I signed the contract with Leeds two days later. Leeds topped Rovers' offer by £5,000 and put me on a £15,000-per-year part-time contract, which at the time made me the highest paid player at the club. I asked them not to make the signing public until I had a chance to tell Sale face to face. I did and I must say the players seemed more pleased for me than when I had been picked by England. They must have been looking forward to some peace and quiet in the dressing room!

Life at Leeds was not easy for me at first. The tax-free bonus for surrendering my amateur status was, according to my contract, £6,000 but the decision to move to Headingley cost me a lot more in terms of happiness. I was shocked by what I found there. I had an extremely cool reception from some of the players when I arrived at the club. There was nothing said to my face but I was put on the back foot straight away.

The Leeds dressing room was divided by a clique comprising Dave Heron, Colin Maskill and David Creasser. The ringleader though was Garry Schofield. He wanted things done his way and if anyone was going to be the star it had to be him. It was quite obvious from the start that I was not a welcome addition, which I just could not understand as my presence strengthened the team. I think there were three problems: first, I was on good money; second, I had come from rugby union; and third, I was a policeman.

Rugby league was very much a working man's game and amongst a surprising number of my teammates there was a suspicion surrounding me because of my occupation. I'm not saying they were a group of villains but for the majority of them the only time they had come into contact with a policeman was when they were being ticked off. The most aggravated seemed to be Phil Ford when he arrived from Bradford Northern a month after me. He immediately fitted into the clique but even though he was the current Great Britain right winger Reilly put me in his spot and picked Ford on the left. This obviously rankled with him and he came over at the start of one training session and stood on the right wing. We ended up having a big slanging match in front of everyone, Reilly became involved and I don't know what would have happened if I hadn't decided it was not worth the hassle and moved over for him.

Time and time again he would have a go at me because I was a policeman and the situation came to a head after we had beaten York 28–9 in a Challenge Cup tie at Bootham Crescent. He opened his mouth again in the bar and I snapped. I told him if he really wanted to be shown a hard time by the police he could come to see me at the station next morning and I would sort him out there. Ford could not seem to understand that just because I wore a uniform during the day I could not be as wild as the rest of them.

There always used to be a supply of bent gear knocking around the soup room where we used to unwind after training. However when PC Bentley walked in it instantly disappeared. This was becoming a problem so, in the end, to try to win the doubters over I bought a suit that had fallen off the back of a lorry and this seemed to allay their fears a little. It was horrible – I only wore it a couple of times.

The anti-rugby union part was harder to eradicate. Anyone who had played union was tagged a softie and targeted. In my first couple of matches I took a lot of verbal abuse about it and plenty of cheap shots when I was tackled. And that was from my own side! I decided this could not go on and opted to get my retaliation in first by delivering some rough justice of my own early on in matches. In my fifth game, against Halifax, Carl Gibson was kicked as he scored a try which was the cue for me to wade in. I was sin-binned but this policy seemed to gain me respect and my problems began to decrease. A bully will keep hitting you if you don't hit him back.

I was enjoying the experience but I was keen to keep in touch with my union mates and shortly after I had switched I went along to a Headingley v. Otley game. I wondered how I would be received back in union circles having taken the league shilling. I remembered how another Cleckheaton lad, Mick Parrish, had been given a hard time when he came back to the club for a drink after moving to Oldham RL. However I need not have worried: everybody was fine which I suppose I should have expected bearing in mind how many people play union on Saturdays and watch league on Sundays in Yorkshire.

Relieved that I still had some friends, I slowly settled into the Leeds dressing room and discovered a different type of social scene. Like in union the players all used to go out together – usually to the Town Hall Tavern, a traditional pub opposite the city's law courts. The difference was the Leeds crew generally brought their wives and families along. It was much less chauvinistic than the raucous lads-only union night out.

Because I had played the game before and was an in-your-face, rugby league-style player I adapted quickly. I was put straight into the first team and made my debut against Salford, in which I received truckloads of ball. The intensity was greater than I was used to and I was tired afterwards but overall I had no problems adapting to the fitness levels required. Leeds used to train on Tuesdays, Thursdays and Fridays but on my days off I would go for a run on my own to top myself up. In a short space of time it became a battle between myself and Gibson over who was the fittest player at Leeds.

Our bleep test results were in the 14s and 15s. This was a torrid shuttle run of sprints against the clock which I had undergone before in the police and which took its toll on the big boys. It was an examination of mental strength as much as physical stamina but always showed me up in a good light. For the short-distance work I was clocking 5.01 seconds for 40 metre sprints. The old pros in the side used to tell me to finish behind them in training races to make them look better but I ignored them which probably did not help me to be accepted. The only occasion on which I received my comeuppance was after I had bolted down a sausage between work and training. You can imagine what came next, which was especially unpleasant considering we were running around the pristine outfield of Headingley cricket ground at the time. Wilfrid Rhodes would have turned in his grave.

I needed to be fit though because the demands were greater. Often in union I would just turn up, have a game of touch and pass and go through a few drills and that constituted a training session. Within league the backs were expected to do as much work as the forwards so they had to be ready for it. Everyone did the same type of training because whether you were a prop or a winger you needed the same ball-handling and tackling skills. One of the best handlers at Leeds during my time there was a prop, Lee Crooks. The donkeys who carried the ball up to the opposition and the speed merchants on the wing who finished off tries from 90 yards obviously had their own particular attributes but their basics had to be just as good as each other's.

The defences in league were also tighter – for a start everybody could tackle, which was a change from union where I played with some England full-backs who did not even enjoy physical contact. Neither Simon Hodgkinson or Jonathan Webb relished tackling or being tackled and they collected almost 50 caps between them. I mean, what's the point playing at that level if you don't like mixing it? They were picked simply because of their goalkicking. A hell of a lot has changed since then and you could not select the same sort of player now. Matt Perry might be a slim physical presence but his defence is one of the strongest parts of his game.

What did trip me up on occasions was my liking for runs

along the touchline which led to me being bundled into touch several times. In union this would not have mattered so much, especially in those days before lifting was legalized at the lineout and you could win back possession, but in league it meant a scrum to the opposition, lost ball and earache from Colin Maskill who used to call me a 'Twickenham t***'. This was what I loved: the sense of expectancy which hadn't been there in union. I was being paid hard-earned money to play and therefore I was expected to perform. People either buckle or thrive when they are put under pressure and I responded. All of a sudden there were people wanting my autograph every week.

Leeds were one of the big boys of rugby league, which was good in that I had the chance to play in front of five-figure crowds every other week but bad in other respects. The game is played in such a small geographical area that the rivalries which develop are extremely strong. We were universally hated by the other clubs which meant they raised their games to try to knock us flat on our faces and it worked more often than it should have. In theory we had the better players but time and again we would slip up against lesser sides.

For Leeds our biggest games of the season were those against Wigan, Widnes and St Helens; for every other club in Yorkshire their most important game, the one which could make or break their season, was against us. For tight-knit mining communities like Castleford and Featherstone we provided the opportunity for them to flick two fingers at the Cheque-book Charlies. They said Leeds had no heart and when we went behind we would never come back. They were right. It took a long time for Leeds to approach the levels of consistency and success they should have done. When they won the Challenge Cup at Wembley in 1999 it was their first major title since 1978 which was just ridiculous considering the level of support they commanded.

For the players one of the difficulties was that we had it too easy. The facilities at Headingley were superb. The playing surface was like a carpet – it would have been fit for a game of bowls. The ground wasn't all-seater but the two stands and two terraces would have been superior to many soccer grounds before the Taylor Report brought higher standards. There was an electronic scoreboard too. The changing rooms were good and became even better when they moved them under the North Stand which the stadium shares with the cricket ground. There were hospitality facilities to bring in extra revenue, which meant if anything needed replacing there was always the money there to do it. Then there is the history. So many great players had gone before – players like Lewis Jones and Alan Smith had sped down the wing before me. It truly was a venue of legends and is still my favourite ground today. But when we went away to places like Halifax and Widnes it was a culture shock. Widnes had one toilet for all of us to share which in the tense moments leading up to a game could be totally insufficient. You were lucky if there was any paper too. Halifax was just as bad.

The crowds used to really have it in for us too. The anti-Leeds feeling should have brought us together as a side but there was too much of a split in the dressing room for that to happen. Players would run through a brick wall for a mate but when half the team could not stand each other there was never much chance of that happening. When the opposition supporters turned on us I was on the wing and could hear every word. It was a world away from rugby union, particularly at Hull where the occupants of the Threepenny Stand were just animals. The abuse rained down there and although I like a bit of banter with the crowd some of it was so offensive it was unbelievable. I didn't even know my mother had been to Hull! On one occasion there a kid spat all the way down my shirt as I walking off the field. He was calling me a pig and wagging his finger at me through the wire mesh that the supporters are trapped behind. So I grabbed it and bent it upwards. He was on his knees in pain and I could have broken it but I politely told him not to spit at people instead. I hadn't noticed a policeman nearby and when I let go of the kid's finger he turned to the copper and asked what he was going to do about me. 'I heard what you called him,' said the policeman, and the case went no further.

The worst abuse I received was at Post Office Road. It was at the time of a miners' strike and there were plenty of them standing on the terraces at Featherstone. One of the miners seemed to have a massive problem with the fact that I was a policeman. Relationships between the two had completely broken down during the dispute. He was off his head, shouting out that he wished I was dead. To be on the receiving end of something like that is quite scary.

The Leeds fans could have their moments and I knew from the start I had to go all out to impress them. Just before I switched codes I remember being in the South Stand watching them lose to Castleford in the John Player Cup and thinking that I needed to win these people over. If a player didn't make a good impression they could make his life hell. Fortunately communication is one of my strengths and I managed to get them onside. Later on in my career, when I was playing against Leeds for Halifax, I could usually detect a measure of respect in the good-natured stick I was given when I returned to Headingley. But not always.

Once, I was getting some vicious abuse from a trio of individuals. This was always a highly charged match for me anyway and when I heard them laying into me I looked across at them in fury. There was a man, a woman and a horrible thing in an anorak who were responsible. 'You can dead eye me Bentley but you can't do f*** all to me,' it said. I stopped and I was within an ace of jumping over the hoardings and showing them just what I couldn't do. I know just what Eric Cantona felt when he karate kicked that Crystal Palace fan. Fortunately I stopped myself and took it out on James Lowes instead. Taking notice of what people say from the terraces is a weakness of mine.

As well as the personality clashes within the Leeds side, we had another shortcoming to stop us punching our weight. We lacked an animal up front. All the other top sides had people you would deliberately choose to avoid in a tackle situation but there was no one at Leeds I felt that way about. Rugby, of either code, is a physical game and it is essential to have some kind of enforcer whom the opposition have to think twice about if a side is to be successful. Warrington had Les Boyd, Widnes Kurt Sorensen and Bradford had two – Kelvin Skerrett and Karl Fairbank. Having someone who is madder than your opponents always helps. Leeds tried it before I arrived when Maurice Bamford signed Alan Rathbone from Bradford but he ended up in prison. We never really had that sort of player; in fact, we had probably the nicest forward in the world.

Roy Powell was a lovely man, the original gentle giant who would never stoop to anything below the belt on the field. Off it he used to like to slap you about after a few drinks with those great shovels of his which doubled for hands but only playfully. None of us could believe it when he died of heart failure on the training ground at Rochdale in December 1998. There had been warnings: he had collapsed in one game for Leeds against Widnes and swallowed his tongue, and he also had a turn playing for Batley. But when he died, leaving behind a wife and two young children, it was like the whole sport had lost a friend.

I went to his funeral, along with over a thousand others. It was a deeply moving experience to see a church full of hard professional rugby players many of them with tears streaming down their cheeks. When they carried his coffin out of the church and played one of his favourite songs, 'Jamming' by Bob Marley which any of us who had been with Roy in his car would have heard, it was a very special moment.

Afterwards a group of us went to David Ward's pub in Batley and spent hour after hour talking about Roy. At 18 I remember being disgusted when the family went out for a drink after my grandad had died. But what I failed to realise then was that there must be a celebration of life in the middle of the despair of death. If it is possible to get drunk in honour of someone we did for Roy that night.

I had come into rugby league with a reputation of being a try-scorer but it wasn't until my fourth match that I scored my first touchdown. It was a weight off my shoulders and I scored 11 tries in my next 11 games. That opening try came at Widnes when I went round another union convert to score. He was a tall, black, cocky lad called Martin Offiah and it was the first of many contests between the two of us.

I remember Offiah growled at me in an attempt to intimidate me. He was trying it on the wrong person – that was more my game. I had always been used to playing hard against someone and then shaking hands at the final whistle and having a bit of a laugh with them but Offiah didn't seem approachable in those early days. He seemed to distance himself. I didn't like him – he was too arrogant for me – but I respected him because of his great talent. He had a massive self-belief, something he shares with a lot of my black friends, and he was an entertainer, but sometimes he went too far by goading opponents after scorching past them for tries. He hadn't been a big name in rugby union when he had played for Rosslyn Park but he was a sensation in league. His skills were able to flourish in a game that lends itself more to individualism.

I always used to land a punch on Offiah when we played, largely out of embarrassment because of what he was about to do to me. When Leeds played Widnes in the Regal Trophy second round in 1990 I recall Carl Gibson asking me the night before the game what would be my perfect match. I thought about it and then told him I'd like to win the game and for a big scrap to break out – which was almost inevitable against Widnes – then, joy of joys, Offiah would appear two yards in front of me so I could wade into him. During the second half John Devereux and Roy Powell had an altercation, Offiah was standing in front of me and I thought my dream had come to pass. I ran over, punched him and was sin-binned. We lost 22–6. He was lightning fast and given some space was a master at using his pace to go around defenders. We played against each other at least twice a year for eight seasons and I think over that time he did develop respect for me because I would never lie down for him. In his pomp though he was irresistible.

Widnes, who were a fine side then, played the sort of exciting brand of rugby that could maximize his value. Doug

Laughton assembled a great team with fast, athletic backs like John Devereux and Alan Tait. They had Tony Myler at stand-off with his big hands and superb distribution playing behind a fantastic pack of forwards. Kurt Sorensen was the epitome of their aggression and they powered the side towards a victory over Canberra in the World Club Challenge. Even though Wigan dominated rugby league, the best side around on their day during my career was the Widnes team which blew us out of the Challenge Cup 24–4 at Headingley in the 1988–9 third round.

We stayed away in a hotel outside Leeds the night before to prepare for the game but we might as well have added an extra day on. They just blew us away. It was a red-hot afternoon and with this being touted as our year there were more than 26,000 squeezed into the ground that day. They witnessed one of the great team displays. Widnes had pace and power throughout the side – their centres Andy Currier and Darren Wright were huge – and the whole side was awesome.

Then they bought Jonathan Davies. At first sight he looked a puny, unassuming weakling but what he lacked in physical presence he more than compensated for with his wonderful ball skills. There was great excitement in league when he first swapped from union because he was clearly a top player but there were a lot of doubters because of his lack of bulk. Would he stand up to the physical punishment?

He was brought in gently with some second-team games and even those used to draw huge crowds to Widnes. When he graduated to the first team they started him on the wing and gradually, as he got used to the game, moved him inside. Teams used to prepare for his attacking skills – not that it usually did much good – but they also used to target him as a defender, launching their big forwards at him. Davies wasn't renowned for his crunch tackling. However he became one of the best players in the game, answering all the critics, and even had a successful spell in Australia which was the ultimate proving ground. He was always capable of producing something special and did do on most occasions. Off the field he was a great lad who enjoyed a drink and the social side of the game. He was a massive loss to Welsh rugby union. Of all the players Wales waved goodbye to in that period Jiffy was one of the most influential. They were in a state of shock when he left and when he returned at the end of his career to Cardiff some people still hadn't forgiven him for going. He even had difficulty persuading his teammates to pass to him.

Widnes put all their money into players like Jiffy rather than their facilities and that eventually caught up with them. They ran up a lot of debt and were forced to sell their star names to survive. Jiffy went to Warrington, Alan Taity came to Leeds and Offiah went to Wigan. Without their players they were very little and their demise was rapid.

Leeds' best season during my time at the club came under David Ward. He had taken over after Malcolm Reilly's departure in September 1989. Ward was different to Reilly in that he was much closer to the players and a Leeds man through and through. That closeness is not always an advantage though because it can lead to jealousies amongst the players who are out of the circle and think selection criteria can be clouded by personal friendships. But Ward's methods took us desperately close to the 1989–90 title. As the season reached its climax, we were in a neck-and-neck race with Wigan and with a visit to Central Park still to come on our run-in it was vital we won at Warrington in March.

Wilderspool was known as The Zoo because it was such an awful place to visit. However we played with a lot of determination and were leading going into the final minutes. Then I received the ball on the second tackle. For some reason I had a brainstorm, decided to kick the ball downfield and sliced it straight into touch. This handed Warrington possession and from it Des Drummond scored the try that beat us 9–6 and ruined our chances of the championship. No one said a word to each other until we reached the Town Hall Tavern. Then Ward turned to me and asked: 'What the f*** were you doing?' The ice broken, we all laughed about it but the damage was done.

In the following match I scored a hat trick against Wakefield Trinity and in the television interview afterwards told *Scrumdown* viewers that I hoped it made up for 'dropping such a bollock last week'. Against St Helens the next week we produced almost perfect rugby to win 50–14 despite having Dave Cruickshank sent off early in the game. We still didn't win the league though, finishing second to Wigan.

What the coaches at Leeds did not do well was bring a player on once he joined the club. Success eluded them however much money they threw at the team. Once the cheque book had been brandished the signing was just supposed to become a world-beater overnight. This was the problem John Gallagher faced.

He was brought to Headingley in 1990 by Ward, bearing the tag of the world's greatest rugby union player after starring in a great All Blacks side. It was a great coup to get him but he faced all sorts of difficulties. A spear tackle that shook Gallagher up badly was widely blamed for his failure to make the grade but there were other factors too. It was bad luck for Gallagher that he came into a side with a leaky defence. At full-back that meant he was immediately confronted by big, strong, aggressive forwards running at him. Head-on tackling skills just weren't necessary in the superb All Blacks side he had been used to playing in. He would have had to do the odd piece of shepherding towards the touchline but that was about it as far as defensive duties went. Then there was having to handle being instantly cold-shouldered by the Leeds clique. They were unhappy at the wages he was earning and would talk behind his back about him. So when he was exposed early on there was no one there to help.

If he had gone to Wigan, people might have been in awe of him but because he came to a club which was despised it made people want him to fail even more and the attitude of some of his colleagues didn't help dispel that. As for his own fans, the people who watch rugby league expect results immediately from their top-class signing so he was under pressure from the off. Nurtured properly he could have been a Leeds great – it was hard to fault his enthusiasm and willingness to play the game – but as it was he withered on the vine and ended up back in union with Blackheath before becoming Harlequins' rugby director.

Doug Laughton at least sorted out some of the changing room unrest when he took over after Ward's 20-month reign. However when Doug disbanded the team he never disposed of the personality clashes at the heart of the problem. Ellery Hanley arrived just after Laughton in September 1991 but even he could not swing the league title our way. Hanley's switch from Wigan caused massive problems because he and Schofield hated each other. In my opinion, Schofield just couldn't cope with someone else having more of the limelight than him. Hanley refused to speak to the press at all because he thought they had given him a raw deal over his chequered past. (He had been involved in all the wrong things when he was younger.) He also had his bad side on the pitch. When we played against him, Paul Delaney was the victim of a dreadful piece of eye gouging from him. Generally though he was a great bloke to have in the side.

You could think what you liked about Hanley as a person but he would always put the team's needs above his own. He was quite simply the most professional rugby player I have ever come across. I have always prided myself on my attitude to training but Hanley took it a step further. If anybody could have afforded to shirk it was him because of his natural talent but he was more intense and enthusiastic than anyone else. His presence on the field was inspirational and both we and Wigan would go to any lengths to get him fit. He was pretty quiet in the dressing room but what he had to say people listened to. Even so, I was staggered when he was given the Great Britain coaching job and later the St Helens position because he wasn't the brightest of lads and his strengths lay as a player not a tactician.

Ellery's professionalism extended to a healthy fruit-based diet which was all very well for him but not so good for the rest of us. It gave him terrible flatulence. He was also famed for something else other than his bottom – his manhood. Shower time was very intimidating for the rest of us when we had to push past Ellery who would be casually soaping his extra inches with a degree of justifiable pride.

Even with Ellery on board success proved elusive. Widnes beat us 24–0 in the 1991–2 Regal Trophy final at Central Park but even though we were whitewashed I remember the game as one of my best for Leeds. I was a handful whenever I received the ball, coming inside for work whenever I could. I beat four men in one swerving first-half run but there was no support and the chance went begging. The rest of the team just didn't play that day and against a big-match team like Widnes we could not afford to be below par. We had beaten Salford at Valley Parade, a neutral ground, in the semi-final and went into the game as favourites because they were hit by injuries. But the final was collectively our worst performance of the season. That was the closest we were to come to a trophy during my time at Leeds.

Leeds had lured Laughton, who had masterminded Widnes's triumphs, to try to work the same magic at Headingley. Laughton was the sort of coach who was never wrong – you could not tell him much he didn't think he already knew. He was also the invisible man when it came to training. He just used to turn up with his fag in the side of his mouth, announce the side and then disappear again. He was a man of his word however. When the squad went to Anglesey on a pre-season bonding mission, all hell broke loose. Now Bobby Goulding, as he spelt himself then, is a fine rugby player but he cannot hold his drink. He had a bit too much one Friday night on that trip, ended up in a fight with Gareth Stephens and compounded the situation by kicking the wing mirrors off Laughton's car. Laughton announced that Goulding would be sold within the week but we didn't believe him as he was such a key player. A few days later Goulding was at Widnes.

It was in Doug's reign that we finally beat the arch-enemy. The elusive victory was all the more remarkable in that it came at Central Park with a scratch side out. Although we liked to think of ourselves as rivals to Wigan in reality we were a long way behind them. The trip over to Wigan was always filled with foreboding. I remember being sat on the bus dreading it. I looked around and wondered how we were going to contain them with the forwards we had out. We were without Hanley who had broken his jaw and were looking at a hiding. Their team was packed with 13 internationals. They were so good they could afford to have Great Britain players Andy Gregory and Andy Goodway on the bench. I needn't have worried: our forwards, and the rest of us, played out of their skins. We tackled everything above grass and beat them 19–0. Phil Ford scored a couple of tries and we inched clear to 13–0 before I took the ball deep in our half, weaved my way through the defence and outpaced Denis Betts to score. It was an amazing win.

Despite finishing top try-scorer for Leeds that season and being a firm favourite with the crowd, I fell out with Laughton and it was to cost me dear. He insisted that a player must train the day before a game or he would be left out. In the build-up to our match against Castleford he called an early session which, with my police work, I could not make. I rang him and left a message but he did not receive it and when I failed to show up for training I was dropped. It wasn't the first time I had been left out – under Ward I used to cross my fingers behind my back every time the team was announced – but the others were form decisions. It was the beginning of the end of my Leeds career.

I was packed off to Wheldon Road that night for the depressing experience of playing against Castleford A team. I spent one game on the first-team bench as punishment and came on against Halifax with not long left. We were behind and Laughton told me to do something special. I did: I threw a long, speculative pass behind John Gallagher in our own 22 and Halifax picked it up and scored. Game over.

Nevertheless I was recalled for the second leg of our Easter double-header at Thrum Hall. Unfortunately I made a bad error in allowing their tiny winger Henry Sharp to stand me up. He feigned to go inside, stopped and jinked back leaving me clutching at mid-air. The little sod never let me forget it and Laughton made up his mind that I would never start another game for Leeds. He thought my body language as I walked back showed that I didn't care. In fact that couldn't have been further from the truth – I was feeling totally embarrassed.

I was left out for the Premiership play-off quarter-final against Warrington which we drew 15–15 and the fact that I didn't travel with the team to watch the game counted against me in Laughton's eyes. Only after the replay, which we won without any involvement for me, did I go to see him. He again thought the speed with which I had reacted was a sign that Leeds was not top of my list of priorities; but in reality it was because he had specifically told us not to come knocking at his door all the time.

After our chat, he put me on the bench again for the Premiership semi-final against Wigan. He brought me on but by that stage Martin Offiah had already run in a hat-trick past one of our youngsters, Lee Deakin. It was to get worse. Offiah scored another seven past me to end up with ten. It was like walking into a blaze at a fireworks factory. We were slaughtered 74–6 and for me and Leeds that was that.

In the summer Laughton signed Jim Fallon from rugby union and I found out from an agent he was trying to offload me to various clubs. It was all wrong. I was a good player and, almost as importantly, I really wanted to play for the club and I'd just had my best season for them. Leeds should never have sold me. Even Doug might admit now that he made a mistake. But Leeds needed money to buy Deryck Fox from

Featherstone Rovers so with me a marketable asset I had to go – although not without a dust-up.

The club were having the usual pre-season trip to Anglesey in August 1992 and I was expected to go even though I was aware I wasn't part of Doug Laughton's plans. The visit meant taking five days off work and I didn't think it was worth it so I told Leeds I couldn't go. When he heard this the club's chief executive Alf Davies told me to give my club car, a Ford Orion, back. That was a bit of a shock. We had a meeting and, despite knowing that I was going to be offloaded, I decided to go to Anglesey. That way I got to keep the car!

Anglesey was an outdoor pursuits trip with pot-holing, abseiling and that sort of thing on the menu. It ended with a big run on the last day. I was favourite to win the race but I was pipped into second place by John Gallagher. Each night one of us would have to make a five-minute speech to the rest of the squad and after I had lost Laughton picked me out and told me I had to speak on why I had lost the race. He was just being smug really but I made a decent fist of it and afterwards he told me he might have weighed me up wrongly. However in my book the damage had been done and unbeknown to Leeds I had taken it upon myself to sort out my own future.

I wasn't going to let them get away with trying to dispose of me behind my back – I felt like a piece of meat. So I contacted various clubs and agreed terms with Wakefield Trinity. Laughton was livid about this when he found out. Alf asked me to stay and if Laughton had done the same I might well have done, but he never once gave me the impression that I was wanted. I felt let down by him and the club and although I had never wanted to play for anyone else I felt I had to go. Resigned to the fact I was off, Leeds opted to send myself and Gary Divorty to Halifax for £100,000 which, in hindsight, was a steal. Financially, Halifax appeared more stable at the time than Trinity because they were able to pay cash. There was also the advantage of never having to change in the diabolical visitors' dressing room at Thrum Hall again.

In the end Leeds missed out on Fox who went to Bradford Northern when he returned from the Great Britain tour. When I went to collect my boots for the last time from Leeds I ran into Laughton and mentioned that he'd missed his man. 'We'll have Andy Gregory instead and get Fox next year then,' he said. He would always have the last word, Doug.

The fall-out with Laughton came at just the wrong moment for my international career. I had made my debut for Great Britain earlier that 1991–2 season against France in Perpignan and scored a try. The Kangaroos tour beckoned but strangely, when the situation turned sour at Leeds and I missed out, I wasn't particularly upset. Certainly, it was nothing like as bad as when the North hadn't picked me to play divisional rugby union.

International rugby league plays second fiddle to the club game in terms of interest and spectators. The sense of occasion that a union international commands dwarfs it. There was nothing like the same thrill from my Great Britain debut as when I was picked to play for England at union. One was a childhood fantasy becoming reality, the other meant having to wear the most horrible kit ever designed. It was red with a blue lion on it and sponsored by British Coal. I wouldn't have paid two washers for it. I sneaked in ahead of St John Ellis, who was top try-scorer in the country at the time. But I had been playing very well and scoring lots of tries and the press had been tipping me for a place in the side. When the

Great Britain coach Malcolm Reilly chose me to partner Martin Offiah it was confirmation of what many people had been expecting.

We were up against typical French rugby of either code – pretty brutal. My first touch of the ball for Great Britain earned me a broken nose from a high tackle. Although the game was faster than club rugby and we had a more talented side it was all very low-key. There were only about 6,000 in the ground. Nevertheless I had become a dual international and there weren't too many of those around.

Having won an unmemorable game, I set off for some typical after-match celebrations at the dinner only to find rugby league did things differently.

I was leading a sing-song and playing a few drinking games with the other ex-union boys like Jonathan Davies and Mark Jones – Bobbie Goulding and Daryl Powell were joining in but the looks we were getting from Maurice Lindsay implied that this was not the sort of behaviour he expected. There was a woman from Castleford at the dinner who had won a VIP trip to the game and I had her up singing too. She loved it. Malcolm Reilly, our coach, came over and told us to be quiet which we were for a time but after the dinner the situation escalated dramatically.

The team went into Perpignan drinking and decided to go to a nightclub but the bouncers refused to let us in. Most of the players began to slope off but myself, Bobbie and Alan Tait tried our luck again. The answer was still no. Showing determination beyond the call of duty, we made a third inquiry, banging on the closed door. It opened a fraction and suddenly all hell broke loose. Tear gas was squirted at us. I hit the deck with my eyes streaming and in a matter of minutes a huge fight had broken out. There was chaos. Almost blinded, I found myself on top of somebody with Taity raining blows down over my shoulder. The next second – as Lee Crooks arrived to try to protect me – I was being viciously beaten around the back of the head with a big stick. The gendarmerie had turned up and they weren't bothering with any paperwork. After being given a good hiding we were bundled into taxis and told to go away. For some reason it took me two years to win another cap.

Being selected for Perpignan was another acknowledgement of my progress. It also earned me a £5,000 bonus at Leeds. Cash has never been an incentive for me as far as rugby is concerned. The way I see it, if people have paid good money to watch – which has been earned in a lot harder jobs than playing rugby – the players have a duty to try their best for them, not the money. To be paid £1,500 per game which I was for big games by Leeds was nice but I only thought about the financial rewards in the shower afterwards. The only time I have seen win bonuses make a big difference was when Halifax were threatened with relegation in 1991–2 and had to play us at Headingley on their run-in. Their chairman came into the dressing room before the game and offered them a wad of extra cash if they could turn us over – which they promptly did.

Since Leeds were destined never to make the Challenge Cup final I had to go by my own steam. Wembley meant an excuse for the northern hordes to pour down to the capital – players, fans, everybody – for a monumental knees-up. I'm proud to say I played my part in keeping the image of the northern barbarian well and truly alive.

My first experience of this phenomenal drinking experience came with a group of Wigan lads and stretched from Thursday night to Monday. We were in a newsagent's getting stocked up for the journey and I was politely queueing to pay for my four-pack when I noticed my colleagues emptying the fridge of alcohol. The difference was they weren't paying. We emptied London of alcohol too that trip and I picked up an injury being turned upside down and put head first into a litter bin.

Another year I made the mistake of not bothering to go to the game but watching it in a pub on the Portobello Road instead. The advantage of being at Wembley was that it gave you an 80-minute break from drinking but this time there was no such respite. There was a gang of us trying to get into a taxi but the driver wasn't having any of it and ended up in a dispute with Steve Molloy. Steve, for some unknown reason, spat in the driver's face and everyone ran off in different directions. Everyone that is except me. I was paralysed thinking whether I would in more trouble if I stayed and faced the music – after all I hadn't done anything wrong – or scarpered and looked guilty. My police career could have been on the line. In the end I ran.

Later that evening we were sat, blathered, in another taxi when I saw a young woman being mugged. I leapt up to try and intervene but the taxi driver locked the door to keep me in. The woman ended up losing her handbag, the mugger ran off and I went ballistic. I was so angry the taxi driver decided it would be in his interests to pull up by a police van and report me. I had no shirt on and was soaked in water after a pub game with Eggbox. Suddenly I began to see that the notorious Met Police might not take my side of the argument. I could envisage a night in a cell looming so I thought quickly and begged the shirt off the back of Molloy, who was also in the taxi. The plan worked and the policeman ended up playing peacemaker.

However this left Steve without a shirt and I wasn't about to give him it back. He chased me through the streets but being a forward he couldn't catch me. In the end he came puffing and panting up to a bus queue where I was standing. People were looking on anxiously so I dropped my trousers, bent over and played the rent boy. 'Ten pounds and get it over with,' I said. The queue looked appalled.

The Wembley exodus will be sadly missed while the great ground is being rebuilt but I'm sure some fun will be had at Murrayfield instead. Personally I'll miss Wembley Way and the mounted police that patrol it before the match. On the way to one final one of the horses dropped a steaming present out of its backside in front of me so, for a £1 bet, I popped it into my mouth. There was a Bradford fan behind and he recognized me. I was too drunk to care. 'How much if I swallow it?' I asked. Fortunately there were no takers.

Chapter 5

Moving to Halifax was beneficial in that it allowed me to carry on as a policeman at a time when Leeds were looking to go full time. It would have been a very difficult decision to have packed in the police in those days before Super League wages. Police life always appealed, I think, because it offered something different every day which would satisfy my concentration span. I enjoy discipline in my life and unlike others when I was at school I couldn't wait to start working.

My chosen career did not get off to the best of starts when I was turned down for a place in the police cadets because I was too small. In hindsight that rejection was a blessing because what I learned in those few years in the real world before I became a bobby gave me a much better insight into what goes on out there. It helps to meet some proper crooks first. For me there was no opportunity to leave school and go straight into rugby. There are some wonderful openings now for promising young rugby players who are picked up by clubs on full-time contracts. They need to be managed carefully but good clubs will take care of their education too.

My first job as a 16-year-old was on a YTS scheme at

Mintex in Cleckheaton where they made brake-pads. They also produced a girly calendar which attracted a lot of my attention and left me dreaming of one of those gorgeous women walking into the office and sweeping me off my feet. (It never happened.) Instead I started out as tea boy in the marketing department and graduated to a full-time job in the computer section. This was rather mundane and when the chance came to move to Refuge Insurance up the road in Dewsbury I took it. I found selling a product that I did not have in my hand was difficult. There is an art to it and even with my gift of the gab I struggled. I fitted my work in around my rugby so I was able to train a lot during the day. This was great for my sport but not so good for the other part. The balance became more and more tilted towards rugby and an ultimatum was eventually delivered to me by my boss about which was most important. I ended up resigning.

Heckmondwike Carpets was my next stop where I was, for some crazy reason, put in charge of a fork-lift truck. The firm had just erected a new corrugated iron building at their depot and I managed to entangle one of the forks in the side of it. After I had finished trying to free the truck, it ended up looking like a giant crinkle-cut crisp. That was my last day there.

By this time I was tall enough to join the police. I went along for a two-day assessment at the West Yorkshire Police headquarters in Wakefield and passed with flying colours. So I was sent off for a 14-week training course in Cwmbran. It took five hours to get there and when I eventually arrived I thought I had joined the army by mistake. The jeans and T-shirt I was wearing had to go as we were all immersed in some serious physical training. After the initial shock I enjoyed the swimming and the martial arts and won the best all-round sportsman award on the course. We all took a yellow

Causing mischief on Scarborough beach.

Probably the longest my hair
has been (you can see why I
keep it short!) Nice tank top
which my mum knitted.

First trophy, won as Captain of Hightown C of E under 9's 7-a-side rugby team.

First job, aged 17. Marketing assistant at Mintex Ltd.

I'm second from the right at the back, in the Cleckheaton side that won the Calderdale 7-a-side tournament in 1985. My best mate, Simon Irving, is on my left.

Lining-up for England Colts in 1985 before a match versus Wales at Moseley. (I'm second from the left at the front.)

The game of my life. Yorkshire v. Durham at Scatchered Lane, Morely, in the 1986/7 County Championships. Durham players John Stabler and Will Carling are left helpless following a break. *(Above)*
© YORKSHIRE POST NEWSPAPERS LTD

In full flow for Sale.
© GORDON BUNNEY PHOTOGRAPHY

September 1987. With Mum, Dad and my sister Sarah at Police Passing Out Parade, Cwmbran, Wales. Mum is clutching my award for All Round Sporting Achievement. *(Above)*

Early international days for England 'B' in 1988.
© MIKE BRETT PHOTOGRAPHY

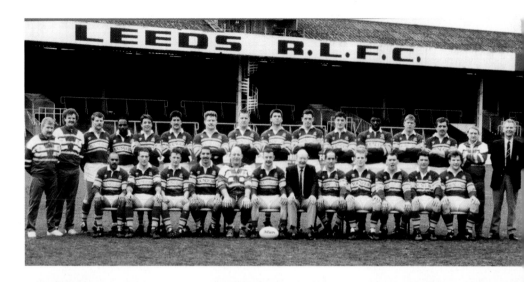

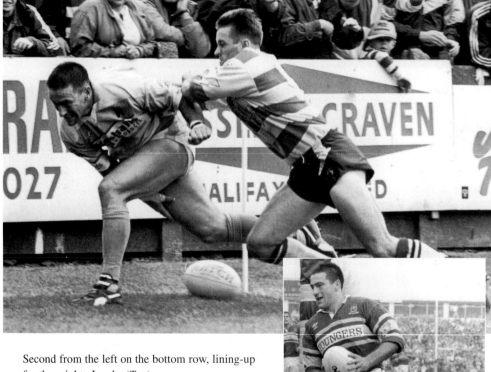

Second from the left on the bottom row, lining-up for the mighty Leeds. *(Top)*
COURTESY OF LEEDS R.L.F.C.

Scoring for Halifax in my favourite corner at Thrum Hall, against Oldham's Nigel Heslop, another England Rugby Union convert. *(Above)*
© *HALIFAX EVENING COURIER*

Scoring a try for Leeds against St. Helens. The try came just before half-time in a game in which we beat Saints by 50 points with only twelve men. *(Right)* © *YORKSHIRE EVENING POST*

August 5 1989. I captured and married Sandy.

Ouch! Shane Cooper from
St. Helens tries to get some
mud out of my eye, or is it
in it? Paul Loughlin looks
on. *(Above)*
©*YORKSHIRE EVENING POST*

Running the length of the
field to score a try at
Wakefield Trinity – one of
a hat-trick. Gary Schofield
is in support.
©*YORKSHIRE EVENING POST*

belt award in jujitsu but four of us had a go for the higher orange belt.

Part of this involved a 90-second free fight where I was paired with a karate expert from South Wales. The bout before ours produced a disciplined, choreographed performance but when it came to our turn we ended up mixing all our moves up and just brawling in frustration. It was like a boxing match and as we sat there battered afterwards, the assessor summed up the respective bouts. 'The first one was perfect,' he said. 'In the second one the technique wasn't quite there – but what a f****** fight!'

Where I struggled badly was the exams. I have never been particularly good at applying my mind and having to learn all the laws and answer questions on them was tough going. It was almost as difficult as coping with the Welsh. England lost in the Rugby World Cup quarter-final to them while I was there. We all stayed up during the night to watch the game from Down Under and afterwards they gave us heaps. I get along well with most Welsh people I have met but they don't half hand it out in their own backyard when they win.

I made it through the course and started out after I had qualified at Weetwood Police Station in north Leeds. Rugby led to me being posted at Weetwood because the boss there was a big fan of the game and wanted me on his team. For some reason rugby and policing seem to go hand in hand. The best policemen I have worked with had all been rugby players as well. To be a good copper you need to have experienced the darker side and rugby brings you into contact with that sort of tomfoolery. Dean Richards, Martin Bayfield and Phil Davies all started out on the beat. The two require a similar mentality.

Both rugby players and policemen have to operate under rules and regulations – they are controlled environments. But they both offer the opportunity for individuals to grab the bull by the horns and stand out from the crowd. The camaraderie is similar, as are the pranks. Officers foolish enough to take any holiday would often return to find their lockers had been broken into and kippers placed inside or yoghurt daubed all over their uniform. Somebody even came back to a helmet which had been used as a lavatory. Squad cars were prime targets. Knobs off the tops of gearsticks used to go missing regularly, hedgehogs were left inside and paperwork used to be arranged in front of the blowers to fly around when the ignition was turned on.

When I was driving the police van with a colleague I used to love to screech to a halt on an estate, pretend I had seen something suspicious and rush out to chase an imaginary figure in the distance, shouting at him. My partner would invariably race to my assistance only to find himself marooned when I doubled back to the van and drove off. A favourite ruse of mine when on duty outside Elland Road for Leeds United matches was to sneak into the ground to watch the match then race out just before the finish to control the traffic afterwards. When cases came to court I always took great delight in reading back the swear words from my note-book. Making the clerk raise his eyebrows was one of the few pleasures from what is an intimidating experience – particularly when you are fabricating evidence! That was a joke.

You had to have a laugh – it was a tough job. I remember policing the Saturday of a cricket Test at Headingley and our sergeant targeting a group of people he bracketed as Leeds United supporters who were having a good time on the notorious Western Terrace. I always feel in this situation it is a case of the pot calling the kettle black. There is no group of men who behave worse than policemen out on the town. This has nothing to do with the police thinking they are above the law – it is a release of pressure because of the constraints of the job.

I felt a little uneasy at first because suddenly, in uniform, I was the centre of attention just walking down the street. I was used to it on the rugby field but this was different. I did not have a clue what lay in wait for me each day but I knew I would be the first person someone would turn to when they needed help. The power of being lowly PC 3395 was disconcerting. I had someone to hold my hand for the first 10 weeks which was a great comfort although I remember being sent out on my own on one occasion to take charge of a school crossing. Even being a glorified lollipop man left me feeling vulnerable in case someone asked for directions. I hadn't a clue where anything was in Leeds.

Gradually I found my feet and burglaries and car break-ins became ten-a-penny. But I hadn't been out on my own long when I was picked up by a sergeant and whisked off on a mysterious job. He would not tell me where we were going but when we pulled up at our destination a woman came running out of her house, obviously upset, and embraced him. Her husband had hung himself in the garage. It was the first dead body I had seen. It did not shock me – in fact I was so unphased I jumped up on top of the freezer to cut him down. This was smart thinking because it meant my sergeant had to take the weight of the body down below and gamble that nature had not taken its course. When someone dies the bowels relax.

I had to deal with many more nasty deaths, including one poor old lady who had died and keeled over on to a lit stove.

By the time I arrived she had cooked. Another man lay undiscovered in his flat for so long that he had rotted away and started to drip through to the room below by the time we were called in. Murder scenes were never pleasant either. My mind would always mull over what the room had witnessed in the victim's last moments accompanied by a sense of disbelief at what people are capable of. Police have to become hardened quickly to this sort of thing and in my case I never suffered from nightmares. The station is often a hub of some pretty sick humour but this is a way of dealing with distressing situations. Certainly, experiencing death at close hand on a regular basis put the ups and downs of a rugby career into perspective.

People react in various ways to bereavement but I remember one remarkable performance from a man who had just lost his mother. I was on an early shift and was just settling down to a mug of tea at 6 a.m. when I was told to go and see to a sudden death. However bleary-eyed you are, it is vital to show some sensitivity. My colleague and I arrived at the house, not knowing what sort of state the bloke would be in, having only recently discovered his mum dead in bed upstairs. We knocked on the door and were invited inside.

'Do you want a cup of tea, lads?' he asked, matter of factly and helped himself to a pork pie.

I continued to treat him with kid gloves, telling him I understood it was a difficult time but I would have to ask a few questions.

'Are you Bentley?' he interrupted. I was knocked sideways.

'Are you John Bentley?' he asked again.

'Yes,' I said, nonplussed.

'What the f*** were you doing losing to Wakefield Trinity yesterday?' We spent the next 10 minutes talking about rugby with his mother dead in bed upstairs. Eventually I dragged him back to the matter in hand. As we climbed the stairs he warned me that his mother was a big woman. He was wrong – she was enormous. I had never seen anything like it and the grieving son even made a few jokes about her vastness. By now the situation was developing like a comedy sketch and it took a further twist when the undertaker arrived. He was the smallest man in the world. I just had to be there when he opened the door to the bedroom – his reaction when he saw the size of the task ahead of him was unprintable. We left just as the third hearse was pulling up.

Being a well-known face did have its advantages. I would come around corners, catch people up to no good and see them cursing the fact they had to try to outrun a winger. But there was a down side too. When I was at Leeds, I once had to police the Challenge Cup semi-final between Castleford and Hull at Headingley. Did I take some stick.

As I see it policing is quite easy. It is about communicating with people, not reading out definitions they do not understand. It is also about assessing situations and using some common sense instead of copying what is written in a book. Textbook policing is crap but unfortunately there are some officers who insist on doing the job that way. Zero tolerance, as employed controversially in Middlesbrough, is all very well but it breaks down a lot of relationships within a community which take a long time to build back up again.

One of the most important rules I learnt was always to be nice to people initially. I could turn nasty later on if I had to. It never worked the other way round. Not that I was a soft touch. I was moved into community policing in the deprived Hyde Park area of Leeds and soon made my mark. I took an old-fashioned approach and decided to bully the bullies. Not in an overtly physical way – the days of the clip round the ear had been replaced by confrontations with cocky 13-year-olds who had their own solicitors. No, I used to employ my speed and stamina to intimidate the criminals. If it came to a chase I would not catch them immediately but deliberately edge closer and closer, telling them all the time what I was going to do to them when I caught up. They ran on adrenaline but I knew they were tiring when they started to look over their shoulders desperately like a fading 10,000 metres runner. Eventually I would put them out of their misery and make sure they knew they had been collared. I never hit them, just fell on top of them with knees and elbows and roughed them up a little when the arrest was made. If they ran for it they suffered; if they stood still and accepted their fate, I would be gentler.

I used to have my snitches around who would fill me in on what was happening in the criminal fraternity. Some would be paid but quite often the people who came to me were those with grudges against individuals who just wanted revenge. Wherever you do police work there will be groups who are responsible for most of the problems. They are easy to identify. There are some people for whom the uniform is an out-and-out challenge and they hate anyone who is wearing it. I found that hard to come to terms with initially and took it person-ally. Often it was the people who gave you least respect who then expected the most back when they were in trouble. Frustrations at constantly having to break down these barri-ers wore me out but by the time I left, I took the anti-Bentley abuse sprayed on the walls as a compliment.

I carried on working in Leeds for a couple of years after my rugby career had moved on to Halifax but because of my profile I was wanted to do a similar job on the Furness Estate. My station was at Ovenden, a poor area of Halifax that included on its patch the Ridings School. This was later to become notorious for pupil disruption and the problems became so bad it had to be temporarily closed down. Even so, working in Halifax was different – it was not as tough as inner-city Leeds. The pace was slower and the people were more down to earth and more closely knit in their communities.

When I arrived the local youths had an unappealing habit of throwing bricks at the police. On my first night I confronted the gang responsible and stood there talking with them for an hour. I told them I was wiping the slate clean with them all and did not care what scrapes they had been in before, I was going to take them as I found them rather than look at their records. If anyone wanted to be cheeky to me, I was going to get hold of them. If they fancied breaking into cars or stealing, I was going to lock them up. But if they decided it would be fun to brick me, I wouldn't arrest them, I'd take them somewhere quiet and knock hell out of them. Having delivered the ground rules I walked off, helmet tucked under my arm, trying to resist the urge to look back round to see where the first brick was coming from. It never arrived during my two years there.

Despite the physical nature of the job I was only ever hit once during eight and a half years in the force. I never used to carry my truncheon – my mouth was my most effective weapon but on this occasion it proved useless. A colleague and I were confronted by three drunken men in a lift in a block of flats. Their body language was pretty aggressive and they left us in no doubt of what they thought of the police. When the lift stopped and we stepped out I asked them what was the problem. Suddenly I was smacked on the chin from the side by one of the trio. I lashed out instinctively and somehow connected, splattering his nose across his face. Another one came at me but he was so drunk I kept him at arm's length before getting on top of him. Eventually my colleague came to my aid and we arrested the three of them. They made an official complaint about the punch but I just came clean and wrote in my notebook that I had hit the guy as hard as I could because otherwise I would have been in for a hiding. The complaints were dropped.

Police work always appealed to me because of the uncertainty of what lay around the corner. I miss that. I also miss not having a warrant card in my wallet. This was renamed the International Disco Card as we only had to flash it to gain free entry into nightclubs.

Initially I took a three-year sabbatical to go full time with Halifax but that time has elapsed. Going back one day is a possibility but my one worry would be the stories from former colleagues who tell me the job has changed. There is a lot more questioning of authority now, not only from within but outside too. Over the last four years I have seen it from the other side as a member of the public. There is less respect for the police because there is less respect in society generally. It is difficult for them to provide leadership with their hands tied. Gently cracking a little hooligan would prove beneficial in a lot of cases.

Police work can be dangerous but it is not always as bad as it seems. I have this lump on the left side of my neck which I tell people was caused by a vicious burglar with a screwdriver but it was actually the result of some tomfoolery by my Halifax teammates. We were on a Christmas binge around the

town and the forwards became a bit excited in Yates's Wine
Lodge. They started punching the metal sign dangling from
the ceiling of the pub, took no notice when they were told off
and of course it came crashing down. On me. It gouged a big
hole in my neck and I was told by the doctor that if it had gone
in a couple of millimetres deeper I would have been in real
trouble. I rejoined the boys after being stitched up and, after
a good night, sidled into bed alongside Sandy. She caught
sight of the white plaster on the side of my neck and ripped it
off, suspecting me of covering up a lovebite.

People often say the police look after their own. Well, that
was not the case with me. I was arrested by the buggers at a
charity dinner at the Norfolk Gardens Hotel in Bradford and
the story managed to make its way into the *News of the World*.
It was a ridiculous scenario. I had ended up in the function
room in the early hours, sumo wrestling in my underpants
with a couple of other rugby players. The manageress did not
seem to mind and entered into some banter with us. I dressed
myself and spotted her across the room trapped in conversation by another guy who I didn't know. She saw me and rolled
her eyes in what I took to be boredom so I wandered over and
nipped this bloke's bottom. He turned to me, upset, and told
me he was a policeman. I was drunk and I apologized but he
said if I did it again he would lock me up. I took out my
warrant card to try to defuse the situation but it obviously did
not work because five minutes later every copper in Bradford
seemed to descend on the place.

I was arrested for indecent assault and taken to the station
in my penguin suit. The officer on duty came in to see me, told
me what a stupid incident it had all been and eventually the
PC, whose bottom had been pinched, came in and apologized.
We shook hands and I was released. I arrived home the next

morning and told Sandy I'd been arrested but she refused to believe me until the papers carried the story months later. I was cleared in the subsequent investigation but it fell right into the *News of the Screws*' hands – 'Cheeky John On Bum Rap' – that sort of thing.

They could have had some more fun at my expense if another incident had been reported. 'Bentley Snores In The Corner' might have been the headline. The shift system in the police used to take its toll on everyone with predictable consequences. Two of us were listening to a transistor in a squad car at about 3 a.m. one night. 'The best thing about relaxing in a car,' said my partner, making himself comfortable, 'is that you never properly go to sleep.' The next thing we knew it was 6.30 – half an hour after our shift had finished. The station had been frantically trying to contact us to check we were OK. We blagged our way through it. In any case it was quite a common occurrence.

Another Weetwood PC, Dave Esgate, was caught by an inspector asleep in his car and given a massive dressing down only for the same inspector to be spotted in a similar state by Esgate a few weeks later. The most blatant piece of napping of all came from two officers who parked up on one of the main roads into Leeds city centre during their nightshift and somehow slept right through into the morning rush-hour. A stream of cars passed by, looking in on the two of them who had reclined their seats and were dead to the world. There were some nights when I would never have to worry about going off to sleep. These were when I was paired with one particular policewoman who had a shocking BO problem. In winter I would look at the rota in anxiety in case I was paired with her. Seated in that car with the windows shut and the heater on was not for the faint-hearted.

I did a bit of plain-clothes work in my time which ranged from the harmless – cycling around the streets of Headingley when the Test match was on catching people breaking into cars – to the horrible. Top of this particular list was the infamous bog trot in the public toilets behind the town hall in Leeds city centre. This was the cottaging capital of West Yorkshire and it was our job to flush out the miscreants. It involved going into this filthy, stinking environment and standing at a urinal waiting for someone to make a pass at me. If they did – and this often involved them masturbating next to me – I left and my partner took my place to see if the same thing happened to him. Then we would both go in and arrest the bloke. Usually being taken down to the station would act as a sufficient deterrent and they would escape with a caution – they were generally terrified that their names might appear in the paper.

It was quite surprising the type of people we arrested. Some were simply blokes that had nipped out for a bottle of milk and left a wife and kids at home who were just after a buzz. I even knew a couple of them. Our job was to protect people who would stumble into the toilets blissfully unaware of what went on down there. Rent boys used to ply their trade in the toilets and occasionally take their clients to a pit behind a nearby pub. I remember shining my torch into it one night and discovering three men slotted together like a DIY assembly kit. I couldn't believe my eyes.

Chapter 6

Halifax is a rugby town. There are special places around the country like Bath, Wigan and Gloucester where the oval ball has surpassed the round ball in terms of importance. Halifax falls into that category.

If you play for the rugby league club you can forget anonymity in the town. You are recognized wherever you go. What had struck me about Halifax when I was a Leeds player was the tangible feeling of belonging associated with the club. It was a very homely place. After we had beaten them at Thrum Hall we went for a drink in the clubhouse and when each of the Halifax players walked in they received a massive cheer. They were local heroes. Moving from Leeds took me out of the limelight to an extent but placed me directly under the microscopic gaze of 6 or 7,000 passionate fans who religiously went to see Halifax. Those people took me to their hearts.

I did not need much persuading to sign, although one of the Halifax directors, Robert Atkinson, probably had second thoughts about me when he came round to my house to twist my arm. He was wearing a light-grey suit which was a perfect canvas on which Lloyd could practise his finger-painting with tomato soup. The dry-cleaning bill came off my wages!

Although it meant a step down in terms of the standards set at Leeds, Gary Divorty and I tried to bring some of the Headingley professionalism along with us. Four years at Leeds had drummed into me the sense of responsibility that was needed at Halifax, a club establishing itself in the First Division, to move up a level. Our attitude rubbed off on the players who had already been there for some time. What we left behind at Headingley was the rancour. In this dressing room there were no prima donnas, only honest lads wanting to do their best for those supporters.

My one concern about signing for Halifax was the arrival of Paul Bishop from St Helens a couple of weeks beforehand. He was a fiery little scrum-half who had been a complete pain in the arse whenever I had played against him. It seemed to me that he had short-person syndrome – a big chip on each shoulder. He was thoroughly irritating on the field, spitting and cursing at the opposition. His ability to get under your skin meant he was someone you would have loved to get your hands on but his big pack at Saints kept him out of harm's way. At close quarters, he turned out to be a totally different proposition and I grew to like him. Contrary to expectations he was a quiet sort until he got a couple of Budweisers down him, when he became more chirpy. His great strength was that he was a real team man and became an important part of the Halifax side.

I was paraded with Gary Divorty before a pre-season friendly against Castleford at Thrum Hall but my debut was delayed for a week because of an ankle problem. This developed when I stood up sharply when playing with the kids at home the night before the game. At least that was the official version. I did not dare tell anyone the 'injury' was actually an attack of gout. I couldn't believe it: gout was supposed to be a rich man's ailment – too many cigars and port, that sort of thing. My wages at Leeds must have been too high. The gout reappeared from time to time over the next 18 months and was particularly painful first thing in a morning when the journey to the bathroom felt like embarking on the Pennine Way.

Injuries, however strange, are part and parcel of professional rugby and sometimes it is a case of forgetting the physio's advice and soldiering on through the pain. I had a particularly nasty ailment called Gilmour's groin in 1993–4 which left me in agony for three days after each game. I carried on playing but could not train until a cortisone injection remedied the problem. Gilmour is welcome to it.

Then there was the broken cheekbone I suffered after I ran into The Terminator, St Helens prop Apollo Perelini. I like to run directly at players because I reckon the ball carrier can hurt the tackler just as much as the other way round. However I should have known better with Perelini. Unquestionably the hardest player I have ever come across, he had already wiped me out when we had met on a previous occasion. This time he knocked me out. It was actually an accidental clash of heads which did the damage, shattering my cheekbone and sparking me out. It took nearly ten minutes to remove me from the pitch on a stretcher with a neck-brace on. Sandy was listening on the radio but unfortunately they cut away from the action with me still motionless on the ground so for all she knew I could have been dead. One of the Halifax officials, Dave Fleming, was thoughtful enough to give her a ring and tell her it was nothing important that was damaged – only my face. She came to see me in Elland

Hospital with my daughter Faye who immediately burst into tears when she saw the elephant man in front of her. An operation cost me ten weeks out of the game but restored my film-star looks.

The gout delay meant my first appearance for Halifax was, ironically, against Leeds at Thrum Hall. What a game. We thrashed them 26–8 in front of over 10,000 and I scored a try and made another one. Awesome. While we celebrated I thought of my old teammates sat in the abysmal visitors' facilities under the South Stand and could not resist a chuckle. Playing against my old teams always brought the best out in me.

I settled in quickly at Halifax and loved being a bigger fish in a smaller pool. I am a confidence player and being the centre of attention and grabbing the headlines helped my game, as did the opportunity to have a larger input into the side. I was initially signed as a centre but when the club pulled in Graeme Hallas from Hull KR a couple of months into my first season I willingly moved back to the wing. I was doing OK but not breaking any pots and I felt a bit restricted in the centre.

The wing suited me much better. After scoring hat tricks in the first two rounds of the Challenge Cup, I waited expectantly for the draw only to see us pull out Wigan at home in the quarter-final. Other than Wigan away it was the worst draw we could have had because in the back of every player's mind was the knowledge that we could be in for a heavy defeat. There was even a changing room revolt to contend with in the build-up to the game.

Our payments for the season had been agreed before the opening match so when it came to David aiming his catapult at Goliath it transpired we were on £850 per man to knock out the holders, the same as if we were taking on bog-standard opposition. It should have been twice that amount and a few of the senior players said we should refuse to play unless the fee was increased. They wanted to hold the club to ransom and I refused. The militants asked me if I would turn down the extra money if the board coughed up. I had to say no. But in the end, after a lot of acrimony in the week before the game, the players backed down and decided to perform.

In front of another 10,000 crowd we played out of our skins and were leading 18–12 with three minutes left. Wigan had won the cup for the past five years and we were on the verge of a sensational victory. Unfortunately I was in hospital as the game moved towards its climax, listening to the commentary on a Walkman. I had given Martin Offiah 30 of the hardest minutes of his career before being taken off with a badly twisted ankle. I'd done my job because he went off just after I did – in shock I think. Every time I touched the ball I ran directly at him, every time he touched the ball I sat him on his backside. I terrorized him. But being unable to do anything to influence the outcome in the closing minutes was excruciating. I could hardly bear to listen as we inched towards glory. Then disaster.

Warren Wilson and Mark Preston collided with each other trying to take a high ball and Sam Panapa grabbed a try between the posts which was converted. The scores were level and even through the pain of my ankle the tension was unbearable. Then in the last seconds Joe Lydon dropped a goal to give them a 19–18 victory. I hobbled back to the ground in disbelief and joined the lads for a commiseratory trawl around Halifax on crutches.

Roger Millward was coaching the side then. He was one of the old school, a lovely man, very laid-back and rarely agitated but we were never going to win anything with him in charge. Alongside him was Brendan Finn, a former Batley player, who was an equally nice bloke. (It was a great shock when Brendan, a young man, collapsed and died suddenly during pre-season training in the summer of 1994.). Millward's tenure came to an end after a string of poor results in January 1993. Alan Agar came in as caretaker coach for two games and, as often happens in these situations, we won against both Castleford and Hull.

However a permanent appointment was needed and after a search Alan got all the players together in the changing rooms at Lightcliffe School where we trained to tell us a new coach was on his way – Malcolm Reilly.

I was elated. Some of the lads were concerned about Reilly's appointment because they knew he would not put up with any slacking, but I was relishing working with him again after what I knew of him from Leeds. He was the sort who could inspire his men to raise their game and I knew I would click with him.

The arrival of a new man is an unusual time for a player because suddenly he is training and playing for his future. Everyone wants to be noticed. It takes a few weeks for everything to settle down again but in the meantime the intensity level goes up. A coach stands and falls by the team's results and he needs to have players in his side he can trust. Reilly was a shrewd judge of a player but what he had above all else was an appreciation of the mental game that must be played to reach the top. If I had fully appreciated the importance of what he was trying to get across during our time together at Leeds I would have been a better player much quicker.

Reilly was a stickler for detail. Before each game he would provide an assessment of each of our opponents' personal strengths and weaknesses as well as an analysis of the team as a whole. Afterwards each player would receive from the coach a statistical analysis and report on each aspect of his performance culminating in an overall mark out of 10. Nobody ever got 10 – an exceptional game was worth 9 and a middle-of-the-road game 7. It was rather like a school report, which meant some of the players would take the mickey and just screw up their pieces of paper and throw them in the bin. I used to read mine assiduously at home, poring over each word in my head. It would always contain a reference to the same failing – 'Must concentrate'. I used to ask Reilly why he put this every time but in hindsight he was spot on. I would often talk and laugh with the crowd during games and if something happened in that instant I would miss it. He felt he constantly had to remind me of this.

The stats also highlighted the fact that I would carry the ball as often as anybody in the team even though I was a winger. It would be quite normal for me to have possession 15 or 20 times in a match because I was given a free role to come looking for the ball. The numbers also showed I was only making two or three tackles per game so I consciously tried to follow up one with another at the play-the-ball to help out the hard-working lads down the middle.

Reilly was a wily customer, bringing in amongst others a Norwegian sports psychologist who had worked with Gordon Strachan at Leeds United to help cure our problem of blaming each other when things went wrong. He could be surprisingly naïve though. Players used to occasionally skive training and Malcolm would not always challenge their excuses. Graeme Hallas once missed a pre-season session by saying he needed to go to the toilet. There wasn't one where we were training so, despite protestations from his teammates that he should go in the bushes, he disappeared back to Thrum Hall and returned back an hour and three quarters later when we were warming down. It must have been the longest visit in history.

Reilly's first full season in charge, 1993–4, threatened greatness for Halifax. Unbeaten in the opening six games and bolstered by the arrival of John Schuster and Michael Hagan from Newcastle Knights we had gone to Warrington aiming for top spot – rarefied heights for the club. During a tense game with the scores locked at 6–6, Jonathan Davies made one of his characteristic breaks past me and was heading for the try line when the floodlights went out. I looked over to see whether Malcolm had pulled the plug but it was too dark to see. We had to leave the field for a few minutes while they put the money back in the meter and when the call came to go out again I was determined to keep the lads fired up. 'Just remember these three words,' I told a hushed dressing room. 'Top of the league.' When the laughter had died down I felt a prize pillock. Davies helped put an end to our superb start with 11 points in a 15–7 win.

We finished fifth that season but I experienced a run in the Halifax side when whatever I touched turned to gold. The crowd were chanting 'Bentley for Britain' and Reilly, who was coaching Great Britain as well, eventually took notice of them and recalled me to the international side. We beat France 12–4 at Carcassonne and even though I played a part in Paul Newlove's try, which gave us an important half-time lead, it was another forgettable occasion. Again there was a four-figure crowd and no sense of being involved in anything special which is totally against what international sport should stand for. Half the lads never even bothered singing the national anthem before the game.

International sessions were hijacked by the Wigan contingent who liked to do things the way they were used to at their club. Shaun Edwards used to run the show. They all sat together on the coach which did not help break down the 'us and them' divisions. It wasn't an enjoyable atmosphere and it even reached the stage where if there was an option to pass to a Wigan teammate or one of the boys from the other side of the Pennines, you could guarantee the Wigan mafia would keep it in the family.

We did beat Wigan once in 1994–5 and I was lucky enough to be captain that night. Karl Harrison's injury and Michael Hagan's reluctance to do the job meant I was put in charge. The icy Thrum Hall pitch had survived a late pitch inspection and we played an absolute stormer to open up an 18–2 lead with eight minutes left. Then some idiot (me) got himself sin-binned by the referee Colin Morris for heading the ball as it was being returned for a 22 metres tap. It was the daftest thing I could have done and I've no idea why I did it. With a one-man advantage Wigan came storming back to 18–16 but, thank goodness, we held out for a famous victory.

I was captain for two months in all because of Karl's injury. The Halifax side had some brilliant backs like Mark Preston and Greg Austin. However a lack of strength in depth meant we were never going to be strong enough to win the league – a place in the top four was a more realistic aim – so a trip to Wembley became a big goal. My first match in charge was a Cup tie at the McAlpine Stadium, a place I would later know as home. It all went wrong. Huddersfield sent us cartwheeling out of the Cup and I fell out with a ball boy. I always primed the little lads at Halifax to make sure they threw the ball into our players' hands when it went out of play but placed it on the ground for the opposition to slow them down. But the boot was on the other foot at Huddersfield when one of their ball boys not only put the ball on the ground but rolled it out of my reach when I was in a hurry to get on with the game. Another ball was thrown on to the pitch and I lost my temper, gave the kid some stick and kicked it away. That was wrong and it wasn't the sort of thing I would normally do at all. I apologized afterwards to him but he had the last laugh because his team held on to win 36–30.

The wing is not the ideal place from which to captain a side. You need to be at the heart of the action, making things happen and being an influence, particularly when the game is not going well. While I always held an opinion on who should be playing and who should not, I found the responsibility of knowing my views counted daunting. The joking had to be cut down too which was frustrating. I had built up quite a reputation in this area.

There was a useful trick from the police which I introduced to rugby. It involved removing the HT lead from an engine – which was to stop stolen and abandoned cars being stolen and abandoned again – and rendering it immobile. I carried this into rugby car parks leaving many teammates stranded and perplexed as their cars refused to move. Karl Harrison was just one of my many victims. Our second row Michael Jackson ran into trouble at the town's swimming pool. He had sneaked off for a crafty tanning session on the sun bed but I had spotted him and did not let him with get away with a show of vanity unforgivable in a forward. As he relaxed with his goggles and nothing else on, I put my hand into the sun bed and grabbed his tackle. Startled, he thrashed out wildly with his legs thinking he had been propositioned and put the top layer tubes through. This made a change from the usual swimming bath prank of pinching a teammate's trunks and putting them on the top diving board so they had to go up naked to get them.

Maybe I was made captain to stop all this. Still, I wasn't put out when Halifax overlooked me for the job in later seasons. The captain doesn't have to be a tactician – the coach can do that – and there are plenty of decision-makers on the pitch. What he has to be is an inspiration. Ellery Hanley was probably the best captain I played under for this reason. He commanded respect amongst his players and he wouldn't ask anyone to do a job he wouldn't do himself. If someone made a mistake he would not give them a rollicking, he would focus on what we needed to do to remedy it. Karl Harrison could have learned something from him. You could never question where his heart lay but, being a forward, he would automatically blame the backs for anything that went wrong.

On our day Halifax could frighten the best. When the Kangaroos were over for a three-match Test series that season we faced their full Test side at Thrum Hall. We gave them a real run for their money and it was only their strength in depth which saw them through. Afterwards they thanked us for giving them such a tough workout. The influence of Australia on the domestic game was enormous and highly beneficial. At one point Leeds had only one Englishman, David Creasser, in their 15-man squad alongside 14 Australians which was a bit much to take. But their knowledge and training techniques proved invaluable. The learning process is a vital one.

That was not my only first-hand experience of the quality of Australian rugby league. International duty with Great Britain included a memorable trip to Sydney to represent my country in the 1994 World Sevens. It was a great trip. Apart from learning that Alan Tait never flushed the toilet after going for a leak or washed out the sink after a shave, I also grew to know St John Ellis, the Castleford winger. It was hard not to. Graham Steadman's brother picked us up to travel to Manchester for the flight and for the first hour of the journey no-one got a word in except St John. During this verbal onslaught I decided something had to give so I left it to him. I was used to being the comedian but St John was a natural entertainer, the sort of bloke who could have turned a poll tax demonstration into a conga. He is probably the funniest rugby player around.

There was some controversy before we left because Paul Newlove pulled out, citing the fact that he was moving house as well as being scared of flying. There would have been even more of an outcry if secret discussions within the team had come to light. Hit by injuries and illness we had been knocked out of the main competition after defeats by Canberra Raiders and Western Samoa where they don't even play the game. Against the Samoans Paul Medley had taken the ball up from the kick-off and been absolutely obliterated by a couple of them. They obviously hadn't read the script. I remember looking at St John Ellis and us both reading each other's minds – sevens was supposed to be touch and pass!

Banished to the plate competition, much to the amusement of 30,000 Aussies inside the Sydney Football Stadium, our 10-man squad had been whittled down to seven fit men in no time. One of those, Alan Tait, had an awful case of diarrhoea and could hardly take the field. So we were left to decide whether to throw our first pool game and take the rest of the tournament off for 'social' purposes. It was a serious thought and we had a team meeting about it but our minds were made up when it was revealed who we had drawn – Japan. There was no way we could lose to them. Taity stood on the wing as a near spectator but we won and with him recovering as the day went on, we went through to the final of the plate and beat Balmain Tigers to win the competition with me grabbing a hat trick. They must have been impressed as they signed me for a stint Down Under a few months later.

The negotiations with Balmain were conducted via Geoff Braun, a Halifax supporter with a golf equipment business in Australia, over the telephone. I'm a bit tight sometimes and when it was my turn to call it took me half an hour sitting in front of the phone to pluck up the financial courage required to embark on an expensive long chat. Balmain and I eventually came to an agreement which guaranteed me similar money to what I was earning at Halifax. After our season ended with defeat to Castleford in the Premiership, I was off.

My four-month stint was an eye-opener in many ways, not least to the 24-hour whirl of Sydney nightlife. Balmain itself used to be a rough dockland neighbourhood where rugby league and boxing clubs were set up by the police in order to provide local kids with something through which to channel their aggression. However its proximity to the city centre meant it eventually turned into a yuppie area and the poorer families were driven out. This robbed Balmain of its rugby league raw material and it showed on the field. During my time there we played 11 matches and lost them all. Ironically the club won the game before I arrived and the one after I left. Pure coincidence.

We had Kangaroos like Paul Sironen, Tim Brasher and Benny Elias in the side and we were coached by Balmain's most famous son, Wayne Pearce, but the quality of the opposition just swept us aside. The thing that hits you about Australian players is their size. And they tackle anything that moves. Whereas in England it is usually possible to target a weak link, the Aussies are, to a man, big and physical. The intensity of their all-round play and the pace and quality of their kick-and-chase game were in another league, as was the attitude. Even the part-timers trained at 7 o'clock on Wednesday mornings. Being part of this set-up could not do anything but improve me as a player. I was rubbing shoulders with the best in the business and some of that had to rub off. There were new tricks to learn from these talented athletes.

Australia's State of Origin series between New South Wales and Queensland must be the most demanding sport around. It is tougher than Test rugby. While I was there 90,000 people packed into the Melbourne Cricket Ground to see club team-mates knock seven bells out of each other for their state sides. Mind you, if you can't hit your best mate, who can you hit?

Everything is geared up to involve children in sport from as early an age as possible in Australia which must go a long way to explaining why they seem to beat us at everything. The facilities are fantastic: parks are well maintained and free from vandals and so are the children's play areas. To work for the council is a sought-after job in Sydney. The climate helps too, of course. Swimming pools are ten-a-penny and Lloyd learnt to swim out there at an outdoor heated pool. I would live there tomorrow.

I was lucky enough to go to Australia twice more with Great Britain for the World Sevens tournament in 1995 and the World Nines two years later when we ended up losing in a bruising quarter-final against New Zealand. I seemed to get along with the place.

In Sydney and Brisbane rugby league is the top sport – it is a way of life – and even with the side struggling Balmain pulled in crowds of 7,000, while clubs like Manly regularly drew 18,000 to matches. The players are idolized and they are under pressure to perform constantly because everything they do is scrutinized intently. It is just a massive game there whereas rugby league in England struggles because it is trapped in the Pennine corridor.

The whole match day set-up at Balmain was geared towards a big day out for the supporters with the main match following on after an under-21s game and a match between the reserve grade sides. My debut against Cronulla Sharks the day after I had flown in included 50 minutes for the reserve team and then half the game for the first team after coming off the bench. We were hammered – not for the last time.

As one beating followed another Pearce, who was a novice coach then, would exhort us to raise our games in the dressing room through bollocking after bollocking. But he was not alone. For some reason Balmain allowed sponsors in at half-time as part of their package, so while we were trying to get our heads together to take on some of the finest rugby players in the world, some joker from Bert's Pie Shop would be inflicting his wisdom upon us. In some ways the Australians were miles ahead in terms of professionalism but in other ways they were surprisingly lax. Players arrived much later before games and generally travelled by their own steam. Training ground errors would be met with bully-boy punishments like extra laps and press-ups so the players were often exhausted. I'm sure other clubs were more advanced but I was surprised by what I found.

My rugby was disappointing – it is never easy to galvanize a struggling side from the wing – and I experienced what the Australians who have played over here have had to put up with. When things start to go wrong the imports are first on the receiving end from the crowd. I scored just one try in my time out there and that came against St George in my last match. It brought us level and the celebrations were like we had won the World Cup. My joy was unrestrained because my teammate Derek McVey, who later joined St Helens, did not rate me and had bet me $100 I would not score while I was there. He never paid up and normal service was soon resumed as St George pulled clear to win the match.

Despite our string of defeats, we certainly knew how to drown our sorrows. Elias, in particular, was an extraordinary drinker. He took me under his dangerous wing after we had lost an away match to Gold Coast and a big bet on ourselves to win. It was an awful game in which Danny Stapleton's career was ended by an accidental boot to his head which sent him into fits on the pitch. Pearce was livid at our failure to beat Australian Rugby League's supposed whipping boys and tried to put us all on the same plane home that night. However he was unable to swap the flights so the dirty half dozen who had booked a big night out went for it in style. Things were going smoothly until Elias introduced me to a horrendous concoction of spirits served in a goldfish bowl. It tasted OK so I had another and then bang went reality. I left the nightclub and was put in a taxi but fell out of it. I somehow managed to get back to my room where I started throwing up blood. I heard somebody ask 'Is he going to die?' and I was aware that two people were having sex yards away but I just could not focus my eyes. To this day I have no idea who they were.

Another torrid session followed the defeat against Illawarra Steelers. I ended up at 6 a.m. in The Bourbon and Beefsteak, a 24-hour bar in The Cross, and ran into an old adversary of mine at the bar – Dave Watson, a full-back whom

I had last seen when we were sin-binned together during his time in England. We had spent most of our careers fighting each other but full of ale we were best of friends. He mumbles at the best of times but in a stupor I couldn't understand a word he was saying, but this did not seem to matter. While we were making up, two or three Australian lads decided to wind up the paralytic Pommie in front of them and foolishly I took the bait and had a swing at one of them. Of course I missed but then Dave got involved and we ended up being thrown out by a bouncer. Dave offered me a lift home in his car but I had enough sense left in me to refuse and off he drove straight into a parked police car.

When the time came to leave Australia, Sandy flew back to Yorkshire with the kids 10 days before me to sort everything out at home which meant, at the age of 27, I was living on my own for the first time. I hated it. It was the silence and the loneliness I could not cope with. Coming back after training and having no-one to talk to until after breakfast next day was awful. I ended up just watching television for the company it provided. I don't think I would make a good monk. With the team out of the running for the play-offs I returned home early, keen to restart with Halifax. I came back a better rugby player and I had a fantastic domestic season in 1994–5, but it was disappointing for me that I was never able to show the Aussies what I could do on their patch.

I did at least put one over on them at the 1995 World Cup. I played for England in that tournament in what was a much more enjoyable set-up. Great Britain had been carved up to create enough teams to have a meaningful competition, even if it meant including a couple of players in the Welsh team who must have qualified by receiving a postcard from the principality at some time. There was a genuine team spirit amongst the players in our camp at Brighouse and we believed we could win the event. Rubbing shoulders with the St Helens and Bradford players was great and England coach Phil Larder forged us quickly into something approaching a club unit.

Sensationally, we beat Australia in the first game of the tournament at Wembley 20–16, which was a fantastic feeling. This time we all sang the anthem beforehand – the players had received an order from Maurice Lindsay to join in because otherwise it looked so bad on television. Then we played like a team as well. The match was a step up from anything we experienced week to week and a tough mental test. I remember feeling elated when the game ended but then I looked across at Denis Betts and Phil Clarke and they were just trudging off the field as if it was the end of a training session. They were right – I was wrong. We had won just the first game, not the tournament. The only disappointment that day was the ground was half empty.

However interest built as the competition progressed and we had over 20,000 watching at Wigan when we beat Fiji in midweek. I played that day after a cortisone injection in my back. Having had my chance to face the Australians handed to me by Martin Offiah's injury problems I was desperate to keep my place. I could not bend down to untie my boots after the game. I had recovered by the following week for the game against South Africa at Headingley and kept my place but after a brilliant opening 20 minutes I tore my hamstring and my tournament was over. I spent hours in an oxygen chamber in Leeds trying to recover but I missed the semi-final victory over Wales and in the end I could only watch as the Australians despatched us in the final. I am convinced I would have been selected for that game had I been fit, which made the injury all the more disappointing.

Australia won the tournament with only half their first-choice side available because of the row between the Super League and the Australian Rugby League which just shows how the country dominates the sport. At international level there are really only three strong teams – the Kangaroos, New Zealand and Great Britain. The division of Britain into its constituent parts was necessary to create any sort of World Cup tournament – only Papua New Guinea, France and the rugby union recruits from Western Samoa were capable of fielding any sort of decent second-tier sides – but carving it up is a shame really. For a start putting Gary Connolly in the Ireland side for the 2000 World Cup weakens the England side, making an Australian victory even more inevitable. And the sight of Scotland and Ireland being represented by Australians demeans rugby league generally. Sometimes the game has to realize its own limitations.

Chapter 7

In 1995 rugby revolution was in the air. In August a meeting of the International Board in Paris declared rugby union an open sport while rugby league was preparing for the biggest transition in its 100-year history – the move to summer. For two sports so entrenched in tradition neither change was easy.

As a player in rugby league people probably imagine I had the inside track on what was happening. I didn't. None of us did. We only knew what we read in the newspapers, the same as everyone else. While history was being made around us, all the players were aware of was a sudden influx of money into the game. My wage at Halifax was tripled as Steve Simms, who had taken over from Malcolm Reilly, decided he wanted to build his side for the advent of Super League around myself and Karl Harrison. Reilly's eventual departure after two years in charge was quite spectacular – he had nipped out of Halifax's pre-season go-karting event early and caught a flight to Hong Kong to meet his prospective employers, Newcastle Knights.

We had a wealthy chairman in Tony Gartland but men do

not become rich by giving all their money away and Reilly had become frustrated at the lack of backing as players like Bobbie Goulding and Nigel Wright escaped his clutches. Malcolm's departure was a disappointment because it seemed to go against his ideas of loyalty. But he was made an offer that he couldn't refuse so I didn't blame him for taking it. The club appointed Simms, an Australian who had been coach at Leigh. The trend was towards Australian coaches. Their ideas were ahead of ours and the English game was trying to catch up.

It immediately became apparent what a good communicator Steve was both with players and supporters. A cool customer, Steve proved very professional. He immediately brought across youngsters like Simon Baldwin and Paul Rowley from Leigh. There was a bit of a culture clash. Rowley was the player used for the naked Super League poster adverts with only a rugby ball protecting his modesty. His washboard stomach did not appeal to a traditional forward like Round who carried a bit of weight. He thought Rowley's ribbed belly indicated a medical problem. Soon after Simms got rid of the old guard like Round, which was a mistake as he was a very explosive player who could keep going at this level for twenty minutes. No one else on the team could play in this way.

The money that was on offer enabled me to leave the police force behind and commit myself full time to rugby. Sounds good, doesn't it? Actually I missed the boat. Representatives from the Australian Rugby League flew over to England waving kangaroos' pouches full of cash at the top players to spurn Super League and sign up with them. Unfortunately I had just renegotiated and signed a new contract at Halifax. The ARL were offering players £100,000 loyalty bonuses in the television-funded battle for control of the sport which was crazy money. Even nobodies from Academy teams were being offered £20,000.

There was also strong talk in the changing rooms about proposed mergers between teams. Castleford, Featherstone and Wakefield were to become Calder while Hull and Hull KR were supposed to join forces too. The fans were up in arms. Try telling a flat-capper at Featherstone his side is to join forces with Castleford and go and play at Wheldon Road. He'll set his whippet on you. The bottom line is people do not like change.

I was surprised by the level of player support in our dressing room for the suggestion of blending Halifax and Bradford. Gartland, who spoke in favour of the plan, resigned after receiving abusive phone calls and hate mail. There were demonstrations too. I was against the merger and believed if Halifax were to go into Super League they would be strong enough to survive there on their own. What I did not envisage was the thin level of support that we would carry into summer with us. In hindsight merger might have been a good thing.

The club left Thrum Hall to share Halifax Town's soccer ground at The Shay and got themselves into financial trouble trying to compete on their own. Halifax's support dropped off from 6–7,000 to 3–4,000. During the summer people had other things to do and different priorities, whereas in the winter the big game at the weekend was something to look forward to. In Halifax and to a greater extent places like Featherstone and Castleford people had very little else. They went to the rugby on a winter's afternoon just as naturally as they picked the kids up after school.

It did not help that the scheduling was all over the place.

Summer matches were being played at different times on different days and the first couple of Super League seasons seemed to be the result of experiment after experiment rather than pre-planning. Halifax chose Sunday evenings but I would have gone for Friday like Leeds Rhinos. It is a good night out at the end of the working week and the Rhinos made Fridays work to such an extent that they were averaging over 12,000 for home games in 1999.

I still believe overall the move to summer was a good one. OK, rugby league took the money and ran but it had to. It was broke. Even the big boys like Wigan and Leeds had financial problems – Leeds were £5m in debt when Paul Caddick bought them. I have been lucky in that I have played at two clubs where I had, until the end, been paid on time, but across the rest of the game players have not known where they were financially from one minute to the next. Not knowing whether they would get their wage was no fun to players with mortgages around their necks.

You only need to look at the success of Bradford to see what can be done with summer rugby with the correct marketing. For every one person they offended by ditching the traditional 'Northern' after their name, they drew in 30 more young people when they became the 'Bulls'. Razzmatazz arrived. The pre-match entertainment was high quality which helped draw in supporters and that in turn helped made Odsal a fortress. They didn't lose a home game until we won there near the end of the first Super League season. That day their mascot, Bullman, was flown in by helicopter to the cheers of 15,000 people. Odsal, from being the most inhospitable ground in the world, was transformed. Effectively a huge bowl in the earth, it was freezing in winter but almost pleasant in the warm summer weather. Although being built on a rubbish tip, it was still a ground where you had to clean your cuts almost immediately after a game or risk a nasty infection.

We transformed ourselves into the Blue Sox despite the ballot of supporters preferring Hunters or Hurricanes. It was chief executive Nigel Wood's baby and although it was a bit Americanized I suppose in marketing terms it was necessary. Even if away supporters soon cottoned on to calling us Sweaty Sox.

Sky invited a player from each of the clubs down to London for two days' filming to promote the re-invented game. I was Halifax's representative in the clip which showed us emerging, filthy, from muddy trenches and leaping past the footballers, who included Dennis Wise and Ian Walker, into a bright, sunny future. The filming was fun but frustrating in that it took so long to produce so little – the set had to be exactly right. We started mudfights to fill the time and Bobbie Goulding produced a perfect shot to splatter the lens of an extremely expensive Sky camera. Boys will be boys.

The game had to change radically. It was never going to compete with soccer in the winter or, for that matter, rugby union which has the advantage of being a national and international game. London Broncos' success has been good for rugby league in England by making inroads into the capital but the ill-fated Paris St Germain venture was a shambles. Packing a team full of crap Australians and basing it outside France's rugby league heartland was ridiculous.

A visit there became a big bender for away teams but we somehow lost to the frogeroos and to make matters worse I got into a fight with one of my teammates, Mike Umaga. Logic went out of the window when John Schuster's eyebrows were shaved off with him out cold in bed. Umaga, who regarded his fellow Samoan as a tribal chief, reckoned I was the culprit. The circumstantial evidence was strong as I had been involved with Paul Rowley and Graeme Hallas in shaving off Simon Baldwin's eyebrows earlier when he was paralytic. But this time I wasn't guilty – although I was in the room at the time – and we had a big set-to in the hotel corridor. We were separated by our teammates briefly but a few minutes later we were at it again. I had visited Schuey to break the bad news to him that his eyebrows had gone missing but my act of charity backfired as I walked out of the room and into a second dose with Umaga. Steve Simms got wind of the fight when we arrived back in England but accepted our protestations that it was a private matter which didn't affect the rest of the team and it had been sorted out.

Umaga had been signed by Simms on the advice of Schuster from the Western Samoa rugby union team. His main contribution to the 1995 World Cup had been in almost decapitating Joost van der Westhuizen with a high tackle in the quarter-final against South Africa. When he first arrived I introduced myself as Bentos and asked if he had a nickname. He told me it was Monkey. When I told the rest of the lads what he wanted to be called they thought I was being racist.

The fireworks which preceded Super League's opening game in the Charlety Stadium, a victory for Paris over Sheffield, were soon replaced by damp squibs. Sky were doing their best to hype up the game with more coverage than ever before but they were let down by the clubs. A lot of them were not able to cater for this new world and they ended up just serving up the same fare as during the winter. Those who did dip their toes into pre-match entertainment often did so with dreadful acts who wouldn't have made Wednesday night at a working men's club.

Before we could start with Super League we had to fit in a final abbreviated winter season in 1995 which was billed as the centenary season. It might have held some historical significance – and at Halifax we went back to our traditional blue-and-white hooped strip to commemorate the anniversary of the Northern Union's breakaway – but in reality it was just invented to keep the turnstiles turning. I scored four tries against Sheffield Eagles in one game as a good Halifax side finished third, but all eyes were on the switch to summer.

The man behind it was Maurice Lindsay, then the chief executive of the Rugby League. He had negotiated the £87m deal with Rupert Murdoch's News Corporation which brought the English season into line with the Australian season. I'm not a big fan of Lindsay. I never felt he really fitted in to the hard macho game of rugby league. He took a lot of flak in his time but he didn't help himself and I couldn't help feeling he deserved a lot of it.

Mind you, Lindsay did players like myself a huge favour in orchestrating the switch to summer. No more training on dank, cold, rain-lashed nights for a start – the loss of a summer holiday for the family was a small price to pay. The only aspect I missed was proper Boxing Day fixtures. Some clubs kept them going for financial reasons but the thrill of playing in front of a big festive crowd was never quite the same. The downgrading of the Challenge Cup was also an unfortunate side-effect of the switch. Traditionally the climax of the season, the historic knockout competition took on the role of pre-season curtain-raiser in its early stages, with the final slotted into the early stages of the Super League programme in May. It doesn't feel right, somehow.

Summer rugby meant playing a fast, non-stop, physical

game in high temperatures and for the bigger lads this was a real problem. With the pace of the game increasing anyway because of a series of rule changes, the heat tested the stamina of the players to the limit. Playing in summer means it is vitally important to take a lot of water on board and at every break in play we were encouraged to do this. A lot of players had to take a hard look at themselves. It was a case of the survival of the fittest and the evolution that was already taking place within the game was speeded up. Players' body shapes have now converged to the point where if they lined up across the pitch it would be difficult to tell a prop and a centre apart.

The training regime itself was not all that different but being full time meant having quality time to rest and see the family. They had often been edged out by my jobs and I had missed a lot of Lloyd and Faye's early years. Having been used to flying in and out of the house without a spare second in the day, the change was difficult to come to terms with in some ways. I need a lot going on in my life and I have an active mind which can be put to better use than simply running into tackle shields. The periods of inactivity put a big strain on my relationship with Sandy as she became sick of the sight of me. Learning how to use my time was not easy. Reading did not appeal, neither did DIY – which if you had seen the state of our coatrack each time I had a go at it you would understand. Sitting in front of daytime television swigging back endless cups of coffee was not great for me or Sandy. She said I needed other interests outside rugby but while the rest of the lads played golf, it never appealed to me because I know, to satisfy myself, I would have had to devote hours to the game in order to become as good as I possibly could. In the end we decided to have a third child. I went full time on 1 January 1996 and by September Millie had arrived – I don't mess about.

I have a reputation for being a good 'tourist' but I'm sure it would have been even worse were it not for fatherhood. I was married relatively early, at 22, and always wanted children. However a slight accident in family planning meant I would have become a dad less than nine months into our marriage. I am quite old fashioned in many ways and although it sounds awful there was a small part of me that was relieved when Sandy miscarried before the wedding. I wanted our fisrt child to be conceived in wedlock. We tied the knot at St Mary's Church in Gomersal, West Yorkshire on a scorching day and Sandy soon fell pregnant again. This was wonderful but she started going to bed at 6 o'clock. I tried to understand what she was going through but the whole business of pregnancy is difficult for a man to relate to.

With her asleep in the evenings I was bored to tears and I started going out with the boys again. It was just as if we had never got hitched. Our relationship headed downhill fast and Sandy threatened to leave me as soon as our baby was born. They were difficult days. When the time came she woke me in bed to tell me that her waters had gone. Being a caring sort I turned over, asked her if she was sure she hadn't wet the bed and went back to sleep. She shook me awake and I took her to Staincliffe Hospital in Dewsbury where Lloyd was born next morning. I was there at the birth – although as Sandy never fails to remind me not for the pain of labour – and it was an amazing experience. My world was turned on its head.

I suddenly realized this was what I had always wanted and I felt guilty that I hadn't understood what Sandy was going through. It was an odd feeling. In a way I didn't want to be there, I wanted to be outside telling the world, but when I eventually left the hospital I wanted to be there again seeing Lloyd. I was so happy. It was a Friday so I didn't so much wet the baby's head as drown it over the weekend. Lloyd is an exact replica of his dad in looks, temperament and mischievousness.

Having a baby around changed me instantly. Suddenly I had responsibility for a little bundle who was more important than me which was quite scary. The birth had a sobering effect, although for someone like me who loves being the centre of attention it was odd being shoved out of the limelight. I did not resent it but I did find it difficult to handle. Lloyd felt the same way when his sister Faye came along 20 months later.

Faye's timing was disastrous. She arrived the day before the 1992 Regal Trophy final. Sandy and I could see the problem coming and having discussed the situation we agreed I would play in the game. Had it been an ordinary league match I would have skipped it but this was my first cup final since I'd switched codes. When Sandy went into labour at 6 a.m. the day before the game, I woke Doug Laughton with a phone call to ask him if he would excuse me from training to be at the birth. He said I could miss the session but that I would not be playing the next day if I did. So I trained. I left Sandy for the 15-mile journey and rang the hospital to find out how she was doing when I arrived. In that short space of time we'd had a daughter. I raced to the hospital afterwards to say hello to Faye. I told Ray French, the BBC commentator, of our new arrival and he managed to slip in a mention of her during the game on *Grandstand*.

Sandy decided to have our third child Millie at home. I wasn't keen on the idea but she felt the hospital birth had been impersonal. This decision exposed me for the first time

126

to the agonies of labour, which were made worse when the midwife ran out of gas and air. I must admit I was shocked. I thought scrum practice with Jim Telfer looked tough. However it was all worth it when Sandy gave birth in our bed in Cleckheaton. It was a wonderful scene. The new baby's cries in the early hours woke Lloyd and Faye who both came in to see their sister. It was like an edition of *The Waltons*.

For me the start of Super League in 1996 was inauspicious. I was dropped along with John Schuster in the wake of Halifax's opening day defeat against London, in which I'd ruined a try-scoring chance that would have won the game. Being left out is never an easy situation to take. Pride takes a battering whoever you are playing for, and particularly when you've reached a high level. But I believe in picking a side on form not reputation. It is the only way. Sometimes secretly you know you deserve it and don't get picked. Post-tantrum, the best solution is to train as hard as possible. What not to do is get tanked up and do a television interview in which you slag the coach off. Which I did.

We were playing Castleford in a midweek game and, not being in the side, I went out with a few mates beforehand. Nicely oiled, I went into the ground and was grabbed by the Sky people and asked to say a few words. I said no initially but they twisted my arm. The gist of my response to their questions was that there needed to be changes at the club – and not at player level. Not surprisingly Steve Simms hauled me into his office afterwards but fortunately he accepted my apology.

In the end Simms did go. He had signed a couple of average Australians which counted against him and the players began to lose respect for him. They were getting away with things they shouldn't have been allowed to and he was too weak to do anything about it. His departure came in good time because the players were becoming stale. Coaching is a demanding job because new ideas are expected by the players all the time. Steve used the same drills over and over again. Coaches have to learn as well as players by picking up new moves and methods.

Super League in its original form left almost seven months of the year blank for players and with union having made the quantum leap to professionalism the idea began to form in my head that I might be able to double up. I contacted a few local union clubs in Yorkshire plus Sale to see if anyone would be interested in my services. Rotherham came up with the most appealing package so, having already had an informal word with Halifax, I put in a written request to be allowed to become the first English year-round, cross-code rugby player. Two months later I still did not have an answer.

I rang the Halifax chairman Chris Whiteley and he gave me verbal permission as long as Rotherham covered my insurance. The deal done in my mind, I went down to Clifton Lane to help out with training and the news broke that I was to join them. However the Halifax board then had an attack of cold feet which led to a stalemate. In hindsight this was the best thing that ever happened to my career. With all due respect to Rotherham, the only Lions you see in South Yorkshire are when the circus comes to town. They are more common in Newcastle and when my old Yorkshire teammate Rob Andrew rang up to ask what my situation was, events took a radically different turn.

Rob had the sort of rugby shopping list that few other clubs could even dream of and I was on it. The side he was putting together was extremely impressive. Funded by Sir John Hall's hefty wallet, he was intent on revolutionizing the old Gosforth club and turning it into Newcastle Falcons. Sir John had a lot of detractors but I found him to be a nice bloke. He would often come into the changing rooms and mix with the players. He loved his rugby – he didn't know anything about the game but he loved it anyway. I think he enjoyed coming along to Kingston Park because it allowed him to relax – the football brought with it so many pressures in an area of the country obsessed with the game. Rugby was much more low key. Another factor he relished was that he could have a proper conversation with the rugby players who tended to be brighter. Because it was less intense, people like Nick Popplewell and Doddie Weir would take the mickey out of him and he loved that. Another factor about Sir John which most people wouldn't have known from his tough, confrontational image was how good he is with kids. He was excellent with the players' children – he used to entertain them in the club-house and make the families feel really welcome. It made for a good atmosphere.

I was surprised when Sir John sold the club but he probably got tired of the battle with authority. He enjoyed taking on the RFU because he was the sort of person who wanted control. When he couldn't get it I think he took his bat home to Spain. No-one could deny what he did for Newcastle though. Sir John's presence meant Newcastle had ready cash at their fingertips and eyes lit up at impoverished Halifax. Rather than take me for a few months in the off-season, Newcastle wanted an eight month/four month split in their favour and were willing to pay a rental fee of £30,000 per season. Rotherham could not compete with that offer and Nigel Wood effectively told me to sign for them. I had a verbal arrangement with Rotherham but I was left in no doubt that Halifax would consider stopping my wages for breach of contract if I refused to go to Newcastle. Some people might find this hard to believe but from a personal point of view I would actually have been better off financially staying at Halifax and playing with Rotherham in the winter. Newcastle, far from being the big spenders people assume, had a pretty rigid pay structure. Unless your name was Va'aiga Tuigamala.

Sandy was expecting Millie at this point and Newcastle wanted me to stay up there for three nights during the week. This was a complication. On top of that Great Britain had picked me to tour New Zealand. With this all going on my head felt like it was going to explode. In the end I told Rob I couldn't go through with it but he was extremely understanding about the situation at home and said Newcastle could be more flexible with training. I still had not signed for them when I went to the Great Britain photocall and broke the news to the coach Phil Larder that I would not be touring with them because of the imminent arrival of our third child. Phil was extremely disappointed, having already lost some big names, and said he thought the Newcastle deal was the real reason. We had a bit of a row and in the end his wife Ann ended up ringing Sandy to hear it from the horse's mouth. I went along to watch Newcastle at Nottingham shortly afterwards and lo and behold who should turn up to watch but Phil whose Sheffield Eagles side were considering a player-share arrangement. I'm ashamed to say I hid – I don't know why.

Just before I eventually signed, the Second Division's other rich kids that year, Richmond, became interested in me but Newcastle it was. They were leading rugby union into a new era. They attracted a lot of criticism from traditionalists for the way they changed the face of the club but I sympathized entirely. If you want the beer and singing and dancing on the tables you can still have it at your local junior club. Rugby union is a professional sport now and the players and clubs have to behave as such. There is a choice to make: the old-style informality and camaraderie or success on the pitch and Newcastle chose the professional path.

As part of the Newcastle Sporting Club, the facilities they were able to offer were superb – they made Halifax's look shoddy. Whereas at Thrum Hall players were lucky to find matching kit, at Kingston Park we were deluged in the stuff. I'm a bit of a hoarder but however much I pinched at Newcastle there was always more stash around the corner. Anything the team needed to be successful was provided. Transplanting the professionalism of the city's soccer club on to the rugby club worked well. Some of the Newcastle United players like Les Ferdinand, Warren Barton and Steve Watson used to come down to watch if our games did not clash.

Then there was the fitness. The whole squad was conditioned superbly by Steve Black, a Henry VIII lookalike, who is a talented enough actor to have had the odd walk-on part on TV. He also writes scripts. It took some time for me to get used to his approach and methods. Everything I had done in rugby league had been very regimental – sets of 10 sprints or 20 lifts, things like that. Blacky was very trusting in that he would ask a player to work to his limit rather than reach a specific number. I was suspicious at first because I had known plenty of characters who would have used this as an opportunity to skive. In fact it had the opposite effect – it made us work harder. He trusted us and we repaid him. He was into power-based conditioning, having been across to the States and worked with their American Football teams, as well as with Newcastle United. Although his shape was not ideal for a fitness conditioner, he was a very strong man who had done a lot of boxing. You wouldn't want to have to get out of a small house with him after you.

He was much more than just a fitness conditioner – in fact there were no boundaries to his job description. He was very much a companion for the players. If we wanted a workout at five in the morning he would be there which was probably because he couldn't sleep at night. I would often find him dozing in the afternoon. Mental preparation was important to him too. He would get players to visualize all the good things they would do in a game, boosting our confidence all the way. I think he will do a good job for Wales in this respect and get a response from their players. He is already beginning to work his magic there as the victory over South Africa at the Millennium Stadium opening showed. He took me round to meet his mother one morning and have breakfast with her – lovely lady, pity there was no brown sauce.

Newcastle were big news and despite being in the Second Division they would attract far more column inches than any rugby league club. I had an important role in bringing a rugby league mentality to training and preparation and frankly that was badly needed. A lot of the players in the side were internationals but they were not up to speed in terms of treating the game as a job. Professionalism is not about money it is about the way you live your life and do your job and some of the top rugby union players had a lot to learn in this respect. They were up to speed physically – in fact they relished the physical preparations – but in other areas they still lagged behind.

An hour before kick-off players would still be laughing and

joking, rather than tuning in to what was to come. A rugby league dressing room would have been a lot more intense leading up to the game as players and coaches focused on winning. This slackness was worse for the smaller games but those should have been the ones where professionalism cut in. It was a fact of life at international level too. Even for big games England still persisted with the traditional captain's talk in the build-up. The players should have been thinking ahead rather than ambling around. Some of the players even ate fried breakfasts on the morning of a game. The payment was there but the amateurism remained. At Newcastle we had a strong rugby league contingent with Inga, Alan Tait and George Graham as well as myself which helped in sorting this sort of thing out.

We had not been assembled just to win promotion from Division Two but to challenge in Division One as well. There was no point buying two sides so Newcastle simply went out and snapped up the best around. The line-up was stunning with wall-to-wall internationals. Everywhere you looked there was talent. From Tim Stimpson at full-back to Nick Popplewell and Ross Nesdale in the front row; from Rob and Gary Armstrong at half-back to Pat Lam and Dean Ryan in the back row: Newcastle were some side. Even though we were branded as mercenaries, Rob chose wisely in the people he signed up. There were no bad apples and the dressing room was a happy blend of people.

We used to find time for a laugh as well as hammering other teams. Everywhere I have gone I have made a habit of mixing players' clothes up so the jackets and trousers are all wrong when it is time to change into civvies. This works best in rugby union where players come in different sizes and Newcastle was ideal. I made sure I got into the changing room first and then struck. Seeing 6-ft-6-in Doddie Weir trying to put on 5-ft-8-in Gary Armstrong's strides was quite a sight.

There were however some moments of tension. I had one big bust-up with Garath Archer. Being hard as nails he was used to getting his own way but one night when the team were out in Newcastle he failed to stand his round so I gave him some stick. He gave me some verbals back. Garath isn't the brightest lad in the world and at the back of my mind I was conscious that he could flatten me at any time. Fortunately the threat of a one-sided fight never materialized and next day when I brought the subject up at training we had a laugh about it. That incident brought us closer and I was able to get to know him better. He is a fanatical trainer who overdid it at one point last season when he lost more than two stones to try to improve his mobility. At his best though he is the sort of forward I love – someone with a lot of mongrel in them who can dish it out when necessary. He lives and breathes rugby and when he was left out of the Lions squad he was distraught. But he reacted the right way, just like he did when England sidelined him, and set about proving the selectors wrong. Garath was one of Rob's most shrewd signings – every side needs tough guys like that – and his departure back to Bristol will hit them hard.

In general Rob impressed me with his ability to balance these off-field negotiations with the stand-off job, although I remember he had a stinker the day after some late-night dealing with Wigan chairman Jack Robinson over Tuigamala. Inga's arrival was given the same type of media hype as Alan Shearer's signing by Newcastle United although it presented one or two difficulties for me. He is a deeply religious man and wanted to bring his guitar along to provide the entertainment on the team bus. Unfortunately the prospect of a rousing chorus of 'Onward Christian Soldiers' clashed with the blue movies that I was in charge of and I was forced to overrule him – not an easy thing to do when faced with an 18-stone Samoan, however friendly. Inga does not ram his beliefs down his teammates' throats, although the way the gospel spread through the Wigan dressing room when he was there had me running a book over who would be a likely candidate for an off-field conversion at Newcastle. Tim Stimpson was the favourite.

Inga's arrival underlined the fact that the time-honoured flow of players from union to league had gone into reverse and my Newcastle debut came against my Halifax teammate Abe Ekoku, who had moved on to Blackheath. There was an old adversary lying in wait at Bedford too in the shape of Martin Offiah – but this time the odds were different. I had always come up against him in inferior teams in the past but not this time. I ran in two tries past him up at Newcastle which must have riled him because in the rematch at Bedford he high tackled me pretty ferociously. That was one of only two league matches we lost that season as we went up in second place behind Richmond.

We knew we were going to be promoted because we had some of the best players in the world. Doddie Weir, together with Garath Archer, guaranteed us possession in the lineout, and was a big personality for the side too. I nicknamed him Fingers-in-pies because whenever there was a possibility of a free jumper or pair of boots he would be in there sniffing. Doddie was part of the Scottish contingent that also included Alan Tait, George Graham, Gary Armstrong and Peter Walton. They tended to hang around as a group because they travelled down together. Gary was very impressive. He was extremely fit and dedicated, a high-quality scrum-half.

Although he is quite quiet I wasn't surprised when Newcastle later appointed him as captain because he led from the front with his performances.

I got on particularly well with Nick Popplewell. He took me under his wing from day one, putting me up at his flat in Newcastle and cooking an excellent Irish Stew. Rather than showing respect for me because of my professional background he instantly ripped into me, taking the piss out of the supposed rugby league tough guy. I liked that. He was remarkably dedicated to the Newcastle cause considering his wife was back in Ireland pregnant.

The different characters made for an outstanding mix. We were far too good for most teams – poor old Rugby were thrashed 156–5 after which Sir John brought a crate of champagne into our dressing room. However with the forwards' strength deciding games, I was often bored. When this happens I instinctively go looking for the ball but at Newcastle this was frowned upon. We were effectively using the season as one long training session to establish a structure which would be successful in the top flight. And that did not involve me waltzing off to do my own thing. It took me a long time to adjust to this. In league I was positively encouraged to help the forwards out by making some yards from the play-the-ball but in union, where I might encounter forwards four stones heavier than myself, this was not as beneficial. I also tended to isolate myself and lose possession by seeing space and going for it rather than heading for areas where the back row could recycle possession. In league there was no danger of turning over the ball however far I strayed from my teammates. It was frustrating being paid good money just to watch large portions of the game – I wanted to be an influence to prove my worth.

To be honest I expected to be an instant superstar in union, having experienced the intensity of league but the game had moved on in my absence and I had some learning to do. I hadn't bothered watching it while I was away except for the odd match at Cleckheaton. At first I used to glance at the England internationals but turn off at half-time because Rob was kicking the ball off the park all the time, which used to leave me cold. It was a surprise to find a few new laws waiting for me. I had to ask Gary Armstrong in one game whether I would be better off running the kick-off back at the opposition or letting the ball roll dead because it now led to a scrum on halfway. To simplify matters I ran whenever I could and managed 23 tries in the season, a record for the Second Division. I enjoyed the new version of rugby union – it seemed to suit me. It turned out I wasn't the only person who thought it did.

Chapter 8

....

To play for the British Lions was never even a dream. It was a place where legends existed, not the likes of me. As a boy I wanted to be an England player but a Lion? It was too far out of reach to have even crossed my mind. This was the territory of Willie-John McBride and Phil Bennett, Mike Gibson and Barry John – the cream of rugby players from these islands. Lions folklore involved tales of rugby heroism acted out on foreign fields where great players became greats. The Lions, as Ian McGeechan was to remind us, were special.

So when the manager for the 1997 South African tour, Fran Cotton, approached me after a Newcastle game and asked how I was fixed contractually to take part, I had no hesitation in telling him. I was going. Strictly speaking I was not available because I was due to play rugby league for Halifax that summer, but nothing would have stopped me boarding that plane. So having given Fran the thumbs-up, I had to tell Halifax. They were suitably unimpressed at the prospect of losing me for the majority of the Super League season but I managed to hammer out an agreement with the club which enabled me to go and saved them paying my wages. They wanted compensation from the Lions, which was refused point blank by the management, but they agreed to let me go as long as I made up the number of games I missed at the end of my contract.

Having sorted that out I sat down with Sandy and we puzzled over how we would cover the direct debits while I was away. If I had played league that summer I would have earned more than twice what I did with the Lions. There are some things in life that money cannot buy, but the payment for such a high-profile event was very poor. It was the first professional tour the Lions had undertaken and in the end we all earned £17,500, which I realize is a lot to most people for seven weeks' work. But when you think of the publicity and prestige associated with the tour and compare the sum we were given with what footballers would have earned for something similar, it wasn't great. The £17,500 included win bonuses for the Test series which we were odds-on to miss out on and a good behaviour bonus of £2,000, which was something I didn't anticipate receiving!

The Newcastle lads in the initial 62-man selection decided we should try to press for more but since the final 35-man party had not been made nobody wanted to stick their head above the parapet and speak out at the risk of being dropped. In the end we went up to Martin Johnson and Doddie Weir asked him about the payments. 'What's wrong with the money?' said Jonno. End of story.

That is Martin all over. Totally indifferent to money-making opportunities like promotional work and endorsements, he will do anything for a quiet life. I couldn't believe it when he took his kit off for a Tetley's promotional campaign, it was completely out of character. Cautious and non-committal, he showed no leadership qualities whatsoever on tour until he got into the dressing room or on to the pitch. Then what he said went. He commanded the respect that a captain needs.

The Lions' first priority was to pick a leader who was going to be in the side. England had put themselves in the embarrassing position of selecting Phil de Glanville which meant him keeping Jerry Guscott out of the team – a ridiculous decision. Jonno was guaranteed a place as long as he was fit. He was rested early on but when he took his place he was inspirational to the side, leading from the front. He was very aggressive and forthright in the heart of the battle. As for emotional oratory, there wasn't any. He had to speak at a couple of official functions which he did competently and briefly and he used to egg on the forwards during a game, but Jonno is quite a shy bloke who isn't happy with being the centre of attention. In that respect he was fortunate to be surrounded by experienced individuals like Lawrence Dallaglio, Jerry Guscott and Scott Gibbs who adopted key roles. Ian McGeechan and Jim Telfer would take the pre-match and half-time talks so there was no need for a battle cry from Jonno although he did used to pull everyone together just before kick-off to set the tone for the game.

I think he will be more comfortable with the England job than the Lions post where he had to deal with the different nationalities. With England he knows everyone and there is a strong Leicester influence. The media side will be the hardest aspect of the job for him. I don't think he has their full respect because of his disciplinary record but then again he hasn't much respect for them. I'm sure his preference would be not to talk to them – he sees them as an intrusion. One reason is their desire to dig deep into a player's personality. Jonno is reluctant to express his feelings and emotions to strangers. After he had been presented with the trophy for winning the seires in Durban, he held it aloft in triumph. But he appeared very self-conscious. He didn't know what to do and looked extremely awkward, desperate to get back into the anonymity of the group. Stardom is not his scene.

I was named in the preliminary squad ahead of the England wingers at the time, Jon Sleightholme and Tony Underwood. This must have been a surprise to a lot of people, especially as I was not involved in the Five Nations Championship and was playing Second Division rugby. Those lads playing international rugby were in the shop window and I was a relative unknown outside the north of England. But as soon as I was told the tour would be selected on form alone I knew I was in with a chance because I was going well. The selection undertook the most comprehensive analysis and selection process imaginable to ensure they would not only have the best players but the best people for the challenge in South Africa. The Lions wanted to play their own brand of football and they were only going to pick players who would fit in. The management kept in touch with Newcastle and the other clubs to check on potential Lions, character-wise as well as form-wise.

The coach Ian McGeechan, the manager Fran Cotton and the forwards coach Jim Telfer were the official selection panel scouring four countries for their final line-up. Beneath them as selection advisors were England's Peter Rossborough, Wales's Derek Quinnell, Ireland's Donal Lenihan and Scotland's Ian Laurie all reporting back on players. After Geech's reconnaissance mission watching New Zealand in South Africa in 1996, the selectors decided to copy the All Blacks and go for a 35-man party instead of the traditional

30. They wanted two complete teams plus a spare scrum-half, hooker, prop, a utility forward and a utility back.

There were no leaks beforehand so when it came to D-day I was nervously preparing to watch the final squad being unveiled live on Sky when a letter dropped through the door. There it was in black and white – the invitation to a tour that was to change my life. Tony had come up on the rails to take a place too which I was happy about but there were surprises – no de Glanville, no Catt, no Carling.

Although Carling officially said he wasn't available to tour, there were rumours that he was holding out for the captaincy. The experience of touring New Zealand with the Lions as a foot soldier and not being selected had been just too embarrassing for him and I'm sure he didn't want a repeat. In fact he hadn't made the provisional squad in any case. They were right not to take de Glanville – he just wasn't playing well enough at the time. I think he is a good player but the England captaincy did not do him any favours and his form seemed to suffer.

I was initially surprised they did not take Catt. He looked a very talented footballer and it was a blessing in disguise when Paul Grayson departed home injured to make way for him. Catt got some stick off the South Africans since he was born there but it didn't bother him at all. I struck it off with him well immediately and he turned out to be my most compatible room-mate on the trip.

In all there were 18 Englishmen, eight Welshmen, five Scots and four Irish in the original party. As well as the players there was a coaching and back-up staff of 12. There was a physio, a masseur, an admin secretary, a media liaison manager – even a baggage master in the guise of Fran's mate Stan Bagshaw, whose background was in rugby league. This was the largest Lions party of all time. Every i had been dotted, every t crossed. All we had to do was beat the world champions in their own backyard.

It was different to previous Lions squads in that a lot of the players knew each other from English club rugby which had become a melting pot for the Scots, Welsh and Irish lads because of the financial rewards on offer there. However playing in the Second Division and being out of the international picture, I had only seen a lot of them on television before. Jeremy Guscott, for instance. What was he going to be like? Arrogant, self-centred and aloof I reckoned. I had a plan formulated. I would take him as I found him but if he was off with me I was going to seek him out on the training field and bash him. That way he would have to respect me. I couldn't have been more wrong as it turned out – he was extremely good company. But the key to Jerry is gaining that respect. Someone like Tony Underwood, who lacked confidence, could not manage it and he had to take some scathing and hurtful comments.

Jerry has a vicious tongue on him – he just says what he thinks which I can't help but admire. He is cocky in that he considers he is the best, which is difficult to argue with when you examine his record, and he does not care much what anyone else thinks. His gumshield says it all. It has the England rose on it and the word 'Jack' – as in 'I'm all right, Jack'. This also reveals another facet of Guscott the man. He has a great sense of humour although it is usually at someone else's expense rather than his own. Cool as you like – he is pretty much in control of his emotions and rarely lets his image slip – he is great to be with on a night out. When all around him are losing their heads he keeps his wits about him – he has eyes like racing dogs' bollocks.

On the rugby field he is very sharp and sees things a lot faster than other people which is one of the reasons why I don't feel he would have made a good captain. Jerry operates on another level to most other rugby players and from a captain you need solidity rather than adventure and eccentricity. In one training session on the tour Neil Back was doing a demonstration of the bridging technique to strip the ball at a tackle and he clashed heads with Jerry. Guscott needed stitches and having to sit by the side of the training field with a huge bandage around his head was a big blow to his vanity. He was just in the process of landing the *Gladiators* presentation job and his looks couldn't afford to be damaged. He was very much looking forward to working with Ulrika.

Then there was Jason Leonard who turned out to be another outstanding tourist. Keen on a beer, Jason is a lovely lad who took his relegation from the Test team magnificently. Many players with the stack of caps he has under his belt might have sulked but not Jason – a real team man. I had a laugh with him after the game against Free State where he came on as a substitute with only seven minutes left and I tried to fire him up by telling him to make an impact on the game. He thought I meant with a spectacular try. Imagine Jason racing 50 yards with the ball in his hands to score and you see why he had an attack of the giggles. Jason has played all those matches for England but I can't ever remember him running with the ball. It says something about what England demand from their props.

The Lions' open game-plan spelt the end of Jason's Test hopes and paired up two complete opposites, Paul Wallace and Tom Smith, in the front row. Wally had only been called up as a late replacement for Peter Clohessy so had come on tour determined to enjoy himself. Test call, or no Test call, he was keen to carry on that way. Unfortunately his room-mate for part of the time was Tom, an extremely quiet soul who never went out drinking. This mismatch had obviously been festering for some time and one night when Wally came in after a few drinks late at night, Tom cracked. In a flash he had Wally up against the wall by the throat but fortunately the genial Irishman did not fight back and a potentially serious incident became an object of amusement for the rest of the squad.

Of the other tourists Gregor Townsend was probably next in line when it came to quietness – although he was not in the same league as Tom. He came across as quite a deep character who at times seemed distant from the rest of us. He is a very talented footballer though and his spell in French rugby seems to have served as a finishing school for his game. Scotland's shock Five Nations triumph in 1999 was down, in part, to the brilliant midfield link he struck up with John Leslie.

Scott Gibbs was a player whom I enjoyed getting to know on that Lions trip. Although we had both come from rugby league I had only ever played against him at St Helens so I didn't really know him. He was a good professional but when it came to relaxation he primarily liked the company of people he felt comfortable with. It was up to me to seek him out but once I had he was very friendly and we had a lot of fun. He was part of the Welsh gang that tended to hang around together. Despite the best-laid plans of the management a mini-clique did develop. The Irish, English and Scots would spread themselves around but the Welsh boys tended to stick with each other.

We had a week in Weybridge before the tour for these disparate characters to get to know each other and this was when the groundwork was laid for our success. When I arrived I did not think we could beat South Africa; when we left I knew we would.

As a bonding exercise it was superb, ensuring the initial barriers between the nationalities were broken down. There were all sorts of team-building games set up by a company called Impact, ranging from climbing 60-ft trees with rope-ladders to stacking up beer crates as high as possible with harnessed Lions balanced precariously on them. When Tom Smith fell off one pile he was left dangling 30 ft up in the air. There were also canoe races which led to a couple of dips in the Thames for Fran Cotton. The management took part and the teams were constantly changed to help with the process of getting acquainted with everyone. It worked a treat.

Weybridge was where we drafted a set of rules for the tour, the Lions Laws. They covered five areas: discipline, selection and polarization, internal/external communication, team spirit and a code of conduct. Discipline set up a committee made up of Fran, Geech, Martin Johnson and Rob Wainwright to judge on serious breaches during the tour. It also created the traditional players' court to deliver verdicts on less seri-ous offences such as bad timekeeping. The boys who joined the tour midway through as replacements were found guilty of this.

Selection and polarization spelt out how players who missed out on being picked should react. They had to congrat-ulate the player they had lost out to, which wasn't the easiest of things to do especially if Taity had just got in ahead of you. The lucky ones were under an obligation to tell the media how important the role of those who hadn't made it into the side was. This was to try to avoid the shambles on the previous Lions tour in New Zealand with the midweek side who lost

the plot completely. Our laws spelt out that it was the responsibility of all 35 tourists to keep their focus right up until the
final game. We were also encouraged to eat together at least
once a day and spend the bulk of our time in the team room
at our hotel rather than in the bedrooms. The idea was to
create a clique-free zone. We didn't want a 'them and us' attitude between players and management either so, to foster
team spirit, five players were nominated to act as a bridge
between the workers and the bosses. Lawrence, Scott Gibbs,
Martin Johnson, Taity and Paul Wallace were to have access
to the management at all times during the tour.

The code of conduct made drinking the responsibility of
each individual. A total ban was out of the question but pre-
match nights were ruled out of bounds for everyone – not just
those playing the next day. We had a dress code which kept us
in blazer and tie at official functions and reminded us to wear
our sponsored T-shirts and polo shirts in our own time. This
tour was going to be professional in every sense of the word.
As we ran through our aspirations together, I picked up the
nickname Winston, as in Churchill, for my stirring speeches
during our pre-tour talks at Weybridge. The boys took the piss
but the sentiments were shared. We were ready to go.

I set out to keep my head down in South Africa and to try not
to hog attention. But events conspired to thrust me into the
limelight: the elation of scoring a try with my first touch in a
Lions jersey in the mud against Border; the disappointment
of being substituted after a poor game against Northern
Transvaal; the heartbreak of missing out on selection for the
first Test; and the thrills of playing in the last two Tests.
There was also a certain try against Gauteng Lions at Ellis
Park. The rugby union press hadn't seen me for nine years

In the thick of the action for Newcastle. My team-mates (left to right) Nick Popplewell and Jim Naylor look on.
© NIGEL ROODIS

I'm trying to say isn't this supposed to be a family game, or something like that! © HALIFAX COURIER LTD

Scoring my first try for Newcastle against Blackheath, September 1996. Former team-mate at Halifax, Abi Ekoku (centre), looks on. © *NEWCASTLE CHRONICLE*

Rugby League Boys unite in South Africa, 1997. Left to right: Scott Gibbs, Dai Young, Tom Vanvollenhoven, Scott Quinnel, John Bentley, Alan Bateman, Alan Tait.

Sat in uniform under my peg at Headingley in Leeds' changing rooms.
©*YORKSHIRE POST*

A wall near Hyde Park, Leeds where I was a constable. An admirer who wanted to share his opinions – probably a young scallywag I had arrested.

That kit. Test debut for the Great Britain
Rugby League team.
© GEORGE HERRINGSHAW/ASSOCIATED
SPORTS PHOTOGRAPHY

In Halifax colours, I'm just about to go
round Martin Offiah in a quarter-final
Challenge Cup match against Wigan.
However, we narrowly lost 19-18. *(Below)*
© HALIFAX COURIER LTD

Soul mates. In victory with Laurence Dallaglio. © COLORSPORT

Team shot at Ellis Park after the 3rd test. © COLORSPORT

My inspiration. Sandy, Lloyd, Faye and Millie.

Flattening Rousseau in the 2nd Test. *(Above)*
© DAVE ROGERS/ALLSPORT

It's mine. Ball under arm, setting off on another run for the Lions.
© DAVE ROGERS/ALLSPORT

I'm too quick for Emerging South Africa. © ALEX LIVESEY/ALLSPORT

Rounding James Dalton on the way to the 'Try of the Tour' against Gauteng Lions. © DAVE ROGERS/ALLSPORT

and a new face was intriguing for them, particularly when it seemed to be at the centre of everything that was going on. I think they enjoyed dealing with me because I always had something to say and I generally had a smile to show for them. Underneath though lay a lot of emotional turbulence which they knew nothing about.

My parents divorced when I was in my 20s which came as a big shock. I took Mum's side. I am very close to my mother – I think most boys are and if anyone else had hurt her like Dad did I would have killed them. My parents never argued in front of me – it was only later I discovered they had been keeping their disagreements behind closed doors. It is difficult to accept that people drift apart when they are so close to you and have been together for so long. Maybe it was something I did not want to confront. When it happened my sister Sarah and I had grown up and I had left home but however old you are, you never overcome something as fundamental to your life as this. Seeing my mum so upset was awful. There is no-one allowed to make Mum cry except me. I can have her in tears within two minutes but afterwards I always feel horribly guilty. I suppose I take her for granted but she is a fantastic person. She never saw her father because he died in a prisoner of war camp in the Far East during World War Two, a couple of weeks after my grandma married him. He is buried in Jakarta but one day I would like to visit his grave.

I still talk to Dad but the divorce made things difficult between us. In reality the difficulty lay with me rather than Dad. He and Mum did a good job bringing me up – I never wanted for anything. If I needed rugby gear it was there; if I needed cricket gear it was there. Wherever I went they supported me in my sport and like any boy I really looked up to my dad but I just found their split hard to understand and handle. The silver lining was that it didn't happen when I was little – then I might really have gone off the rails.

Dad came out on the Lions tour with his new partner Sue and kept himself at a distance but we met up from time to time. I was wary at first when he said he was heading for South Africa because I did not want him around all the time, but it was me who ended up looking for him and we got on quite well. I saw him cry for the first time in my life on that tour. He had been out of contact for a few days and I had to pass on the news that his mother had died back home. That was very difficult for us both. I show emotion a lot more easily than my father. I am able to hold, kiss and cuddle my three children and tell them how much I love them in a way that he never was. Hopefully I will always be able to do so and be there for them whenever they need to talk. The kids crossed off the days when I was away and sent me pictures they had drawn in the post during the tour. Without their support and that of Sandy I would never have been able to complete the trip.

The welcome from the South Africans was amazing when we touched down after a first-class flight from London. Everywhere we went there seemed to be dancers to greet us. The people in the street all had the same message for us which boiled down to: 'You are the Lions. You are fantastic. You are amazing. You are going to get your arses kicked.' There was never any animosity from the South Africans, just a deep-seated belief in Springbok superiority. That was what acted as our inspiration.

The first three games of the tour were supposed to be the easy ones but we went 11–10 down in the opener against Eastern Province before pulling away to win 11–39. I was supposed to play in the game but injured my toe colliding with Austin Healey in training. I missed the next two sessions and only found out afterwards that the management were close to sending me home because of this. The doctor, James Robson, saved my skin by telling me in a conspiratorial sort of way that he thought it was important I trained the next day. I did and the injury eased off enough for me to be able to play against Border in the second match of the tour. We misfired badly and scraped home 18–14 in an East London swamp and I ran in my first try of the tour but the injury still gave me trouble after the game.

In matches the adrenaline masks some of the pain, especially in a match as important as a British Lions debut. The occasion enables you to rise above it. If I take my tape off my wrists straight after a game I don't feel it but if I leave it until I have returned to a normal psychological state, ripping hairs out has me squealing. Equally those knocks and kicks I take during a game do not cause me anywhere near the pain they would if I took them walking down the street. This feeling of indestructibility sometimes persuades players to play with injuries when they should not. You have to be hard but the body is usually telling you something when it is giving out pain. Fortunately with this particular injury there was no long-term damage. It would have been hard to handle if I had gone home without wearing a Lions jersey. I mean, what would they have done without their entertainments officer?

The job came about like this. Pre-tour the players discussed what we would need in terms of distractions and Jonno said we had to pick someone to do the job. I didn't want to do it. When it was being discussed I purposefully slunk back into my chair. I could see what was coming but I wanted to be focused on my rugby not social antics. This time I didn't want to be remembered for what I had done off the field rather than on it. Unfortunately I was to have no say in the matter. Half a dozen of the lads shouted my name and everyone else agreed, so I reluctantly accepted the role. I said I would need some help and set about selecting my team. It was apparent from the start how outspoken Guscott was. If he didn't want to do something he didn't do it. If there was something he didn't like he would make sure everyone else knew about it. He would always look for the worst in something – basically he was a big moaner but very influential with it. The last thing I wanted was to be suggesting options for the lads and having Guscott sat at the back taking the piss out of them. So I approached him to come on to the team. He burst out laughing and gleefully accepted, knowing full well why I had done it. In team meetings we would spend 20 minutes mulling over a certain plan and then he would wade in and write off the whole thing, refusing to do it. To make it worse he would instantly come up with a better scheme. That's Guscott for you.

My other two picks were Scott Gibbs – to get the Welsh lads on board – and Doddie Weir because he liked to be involved in everything. When he went home injured I didn't bother with a replacement because he hadn't done anything anyway. I thought about co-opting Rob Wainwright but decided against it because his idea of fun wouldn't have gone down well with the rest of the team. One day he took a load of them out for a two-hour ramble! Falconry was his scene and myself and Dai Young used to make budgie noises when he walked past. I don't think he sussed.

The job was quite easy. All we had to do was to keep a constant flow of activities available. Golf, go-karting, cinema, pornography . . . all tastes were catered for. I was the porn librarian which provided me with an interesting insight into different players' interests. There were browsers and there were hoarders. Some would like a magazine pushed quietly under their doors while others went the whole hog and took the television and video out of the team room to view tapes that had nothing to do with rugby. Actually, that was me – although Jason Leonard was guilty too. There was one extremely tame magazine called *Barely Legal* which we purchased near the start of the tour that survived right until the end. It was in a very poor condition through over-use by then. As far as I'm concerned the porn was an essential element of the tour – seven weeks away from wives and girl-friends is a long time. You can categorize men into two groups – wankers and liars. I actually caught two of the Lions in the act when I was filming for the tour video but to protect their embarrassment I won't mention Barry Williams or Austin Healey by name.

Very little was compulsory – only a team trip to a restaurant every Thursday evening. The traditional tour court session also sat, though in a less alcoholic fashion than in the amateur days with Judge Keith Wood delivering summary justice in an appalling wig. Only the coaches suffered with alcohol – poor old Geech had to down the largest whisky you've ever seen in one gulp. Fran, who was accused of giving the same speech too often, was tried and found guilty for being boring on tour after some poor work from his defence counsel Mark Regan. Austin was tied up with tape and had an apple stuffed into his mouth like the Gimp in *Pulp Fiction* for being Austin. On previous Lions tours they seemed to have proper singers but as we didn't we had a tour tune – 'Wonderwall' by Oasis – which we could all wail. We seemed to hear it every time we did well. It was an OK song and it helped to bring us together but we could have chosen a better band. I hate Oasis. They seem to think everybody owes them something. Who do they think they are? They don't give a damn. In my opinion they could do with a right good hiding. Rather like James Small.

My second match on tour after the slog through the mud against Border became notorious. Before we flew out Va'aiga Tuigamala told me if I only did one thing on tour it should be to kick Small's backside. He rated Small as the best player he had come up against but also the most irritating. When I saw Inga again afterwards he laughed and said he had not meant it literally. Small, the playboy of South African rugby, had been built up by the Lions management in the days leading up to the Western Province game as a superstar and to be honest I was a bit sick of it all. I was down to play left wing and mark him – whether that was a deliberate ploy I don't know – but I told Jason Leonard that Small had it coming to him.

The situation did not look good at first. He left me standing with a beautiful piece of football when he took me on the outside and as he came past after just failing to score with a chip and chase he left me in no doubt how pleased about it he was. So did the crowd in Cape Town. My initial wish was for the ground to swallow me up and in the past I would have retreated into my shell and become scared to get involved. But I took a deep breath, told myself he was not going to do that to me and made a conscious effort to involve myself as soon as I possibly could. The next time Small had possession, he had no room and I took him into touch and headbutted him. Not a real Glasgow kiss, more of an unaffectionate rub of the head across his face. That upset him and we had to be separated. Then he took a high ball, was wrapped up and I was all over him like a rash. I had my forearm in his face and was roughing him up but when he emerged he accused me of going for his eyes with my fingers – gouging. I took time out at the next break in play to say to him I had not touched his eyes intentionally but two days later he made the accusation in public.

This is something I feel very strongly about and his accusations were completely unfounded. I have never gouged a player. I am deliberately physical but there are some things which are beyond the bounds of acceptability. I was never cited for the incident and I told Small what I thought of his actions in going public after the first Test. He was defensive about it and when I went to talk to him at Twickenham after the England v. South Africa match the following season he did not want to know me. I could tell he was uncomfortable and I made an effort to be friendly but he just snubbed me. I could have smacked him there and then in the Rose Room.

In actual fact I was the one who should have felt put out. I was gouged twice on that tour by Andre Venter, the Springbok flanker. The incidents happened in the Second and Third Tests and I was pretty disappointed by his attitude. You knew when you went down on the floor you were in for a kicking – this was South Africa after all – but that can blind someone. It happened to me once as well in rugby league playing against Dewsbury for Leeds. It wound me up so much I took the ball up from the next play and aimed straight at the culprit. Unfortunately he had two of his mates with him and I was gang tackled into next week. So much for justice.

My criminal record consists of two sendings-off which is high for a winger. The first came during a Challenge Cup tie for Halifax against Sheffield Eagles. I broke Lynton Stott's nose with a high tackle which kicked off a big punch-up and I had to go. It wasn't intentional but as Stott broke down one wing I hurtled down the slope at Thrum Hall and he went inside me as I overran him. I instinctively stuck out an arm and caught him across his face. It was the first time I had been sent off and I felt I had let the side down as I took my shower alone. However the lads won and picked up Leeds in the draw for the next round, a tie I was desperate to play in. At my disciplinary hearing I stressed that I had never been sent off in 23 years of playing rugby and was confident I would escape a ban. Unfortunately they had a copy of my sin-bin record, which was shocking, and I was suspended for a game and fined £150. I appealed, conducted my own defence and got the ban overturned and my fine doubled. It didn't do much good though – we lost to Leeds.

I was sent off when I returned to rugby union as well for punching Andy Smallwood, the Coventry winger. I had been held back a couple of times during the game, which was one of Newcastle's rare defeats, and when it happened a third time I snapped and slotted him. It might not have been so bad if I hadn't followed it up with a couple more when he collapsed in a ball on the ground. The Coventry fans loved it when I was shown the red card, particularly when I went off up the wrong tunnel, and I was roundly abused and spat at as I walked past the main stand. That dismissal cost me a 30-day suspension, free time which I used wisely in having a vasectomy carried out.

The most graphic illustration of South African brutality came when Marius Bosman karate-kicked Doddie Weir out of the tour in Witbank. He just went straight for Doddie's knee, tore the ligaments and could have ended his career. A fine of £1,500 was a disgrace. That incident and the departure of such a lovely guy as Doddie completely overshadowed the

64–14 thrashing of Mpumalanga as the side began to come together in the third game.

Scott Gibbs, probably the player of the Lions tour, ran into trouble with the authorities when we headed for the high veldt and Northern Transvaal. He was suspended for a match after throwing a punch in a typically destructive tackle. Snake's aggressive attitude, typified when he charged at the awesome Os du Randt in the Second Test and left him dazed, was just what northern hemisphere rugby needed from its backs. For too long it had been the forwards who had been expected to show all the balls while their colleagues waited with hankies in their pockets for a run now and again. Scott Gibbs changed all that. His bull-like charges and thunderous tackles were in complete contrast to his off-field demeanour where he was a bit dopey really. His glasses made him look like an intellectual but he was usually slow on the uptake. I had to explain my jokes for him.

In a way it was my fault that Snake was banned against Northern Transvaal as he was only on the pitch because I had been substituted. I had played a poor game and we went down to a 35–30 defeat against a half-strength Blue Bulls line-up. It did not bode well for the rest of the tour for either myself or the team. Playing at altitude at Loftus Versfeld in Pretoria presented no problems other than the ball travelled further through the air. It was the training which was more difficult – sometimes it felt like I could not get any air into my lungs. The sessions themselves were excellent, very intense, and working under Ian McGeechan was a joy. He drilled into us the maxim that we should never come off the field thinking, 'What if?' Always be prepared to try.

His background work in going out to South Africa and watching how the All Blacks won there was crucial. The analysis of the opposition was top-notch and McGeechan knew just what was required. They were good at the set-piece and at head-on confrontation whether it was with the ball or in the tackle. Logically, he decided we had to pick a mobile back row and pack and move the ball around, keeping it away from the South African strengths. He was not afraid to call in advice from the rugby league contingent especially when it came to aggressive defence. We were constantly trying to fill the holes that the South Africa runners wanted to use and we employed a method called the scorpion's tail. This involved drifting out across the field with the furthest man away moving forward at the same time to close down the space for which the South Africans were aiming.

One of the main things Alan Tait, Scott Gibbs and I brought to the Lions from rugby league was the importance of talking. Communication is vital in aligning defences, which the Lions prided themselves on, but also in keeping teammates going. From a player in my position, verbal encouragement can act as recognition of just how hard the forwards are working. McGeechan had an easy job in that he had the best players in Britain and Ireland to work with. We could all pass and catch a ball. What he was exceptional at doing was delivering speeches and conveying the importance of what we were involved in. He obviously put a lot of time into them and they were extremely emotional and inspirational for us all. I don't mind admitting I cried during them.

Geech complemented well his fellow Scot Jim Telfer who, I had heard from Doddie Weir before the tour, was a nightmare to work with. Doddie, of course, is a forward and, standing watching our big lads smash into the scrummaging machine time after time after their poor showing in that area early in the tour, I could see why his judgement might have been coloured. Jim's pride had been hurt and he made sure there and then that the problem was sorted out. Those sessions enabled us to cope with the physical presence of du Randt and co. Jim did a fantastic job.

Even dinner was meticulously assessed by experts. What we ate was controlled by Dave McLean, the fitness advisor. His brief was to reduce our fat levels by two per cent before the first Test so the food was all low fat and high carbohydrate which became boring after a time. You can only take so much cauliflower cheese and baked potato. The boys often sneaked off to buy their own food elsewhere. The search for a piece of cheesecake became like a mission to find the Holy Grail. We might have been Lions but we were only human.

Chapter 9

Tries are the bread and butter of a winger's life. Dogs chase cats, strikers score goals, wingers score tries. I enjoy the feeling although this will always depend on the context of the team's position in a match. That is why my try against Gauteng at Ellis Park for the Lions was the most important of my career. That victory, coming as it did at altitude after the defeat by Northern Transvaal, put the tour back on the road. If we had lost there was a chance that the tour could slide away from us but we pulled off the win, devoured the Natal Sharks three days later and the rest is history.

Gauteng were one of South Africa's Super-12 representatives, having changed their name from Transvaal. Traditionally they were one of the strong suits of South African rugby, comprised of hard men who took no prisoners. Like the other South African provinces they were told to start without their Test players on the orders of the selectors to save them for the internationals. They still had a pretty handy line-up though with Pieter Hendriks, the World Cup winger, facing me.

I used to spend 10 minutes on the morning of a game

jotting down what my aims for the match were. That was something I had picked up from Malcolm Reilly. I would put down key words like 'defence', 'enthusiasm' and always end with 'enjoy' – if you are doing that you are halfway there. Before the Gauteng game my approach was slightly different. I slept. It was an evening kick-off and I didn't get up until after miday which was a delicious luxury after having three kids to act as alarm clocks back home. The backs who were playing that night had a gentle run out in the afternoon and then I just chilled out ahead of the game. That tour was probably the first time I learned to relax – the first time I really learned to enjoy my own company. Mind you, who wouldn't after putting up with Dai Young's bedtime chat and Keith Wood's terrible snoring?

When we arrived at the ground I immediately fell for Ellis Park, the venue for the 1995 World Cup final. It was a beautiful stadium, rising high into the Johannesburg sky. The pitch wasn't in the best of conditions though. We expected a tough night and we got it. Our forwards kept us in the game but Mike Catt, who had replaced Paul Grayson early in the tour, had an off day with his kicking and with 15 minutes left we held a slender 10–9 advantage. The game was precariously balanced. Then it happened.

Neil Jenkins, at full-back, picked up a stray kick and passed it to me in centre-field five metres outside my own 22. McGeechan had given us a free hand to attack from wherever if we thought it was on, so I did. With two forwards in front of me I headed out to the right and away from Krause and Dalton. Suddenly I was in space. Du Toit, the full-back, came hurtling across so I was forced to cut back inside. It wasn't a side-step – I don't use those – just a swivel of the hips and change of direction. Another one then took me inside two more defenders and into the Gauteng 22. I skipped away from a tap tackle and pinned my ears back for the posts. Two more tacklers were closing in fast but I dived for the line and even though they both hit me at once my momentum took me over for the try.

If it had been soccer, I would have headed for the corner flag, done a back-flip and a little dance and then been dived upon by my teammates. It being rugby Catty, Jenks and Barry Williams said well done. In any case I was exhausted. The emotional scenes were saved for the tunnel on the way back to the dressing rooms after we had held on for a 20–14 victory. All the tour party joined in. A defining moment of the tour, said Fran. I don't think it was my best try ever though. Alan Tait told the press afterwards that I scored tries like that every week in rugby league which wasn't quite true, but there were some good ones.

My favourite was for Halifax against Warrington in 1994. We were 16–10 up at the time and in many ways the Gauteng score was a carbon copy. Again it stemmed from a deep kick which was picked up by our full-back Steve Hampson who passed it to me in my own half. Once more I went round the first layer of defence and headed towards the right touchline, only this time I took the rest of the defence on the outside including Jonathan Davies rather than cutting back inside. I finished off in the corner.

In terms of distance that is beaten by a try I scored for Leeds against Wigan in the 1990–1 season when we beat them at Central Park. I took the ball in my own 22 and crabbed my way across it from right to left. I spotted a gap and handed off Sam Panapa to go through it. Suddenly the breakout was on and I was surrounded by fresh air. I crossed the halfway line and looked inside for support but found

Denis Betts covering Simon Irving so I went alone, stepped inside Hampson, then a Wigan player, and outpaced the cover to score.

There was another spectacular one for Leeds against Wakefield Trinity from 70 metres out at Belle Vue. I slipped fielding a kick in my own half but got the pass away only to find us going backwards. So I followed the play from the right wing, took a pass from Paul Delaney on the left side of the field and straightened the line of attack, accelerating through the cover. Seven defenders later, after an arcing run, I handed off the last covering tackler to score to the right of the posts.

The following match against St Helens my purple patch continued with another try which was not from quite such long range but was more important in terms of the match. We were reduced to 12 men by a sending off and were 14–10 down as half-time approached. I came in off my wing and took a pass at pace from Gary Divorty at a play-the-ball and exploded between Shane Cooper and Roy Haggerty 40 metres out. My angle took me outside Phil Veivers and I cut back inside Brimah Kebbie to score. A packed house at Headingley went bananas and the goal took us into the interval 16–14 up. We never looked back and had run up a half-century by the end of the game.

Aside from the Gauteng touchdown, my next most memorable score in union was from only about 30 metres out but it rounded off a fine match for me. It came before I switched to rugby league, for Yorkshire against Durham at Morley in the 1986–7 county championship. What gave me the greatest satisfaction was that it involved me going outside Durham's David Cooke, a real flier on the wing, whom Mike Harrison had not managed to get past all afternoon.

I could have had another long-range cracker against the

Emerging Springboks in the last game before the first Test on the Lions tour but instead I passed to Nick Beal who touched down. Yet the 60-metre run and the storming try against Gauteng failed to earn me a place in the Test side.

The nearest anyone came to going 'off tour' was probably me after the disappointment of missing out. I was in charge of a mini video camera for the 'Living with Lions' fly-on-the-wall documentary when the time arrived for selection. This was my idea as I thought it would help the makers get some more entertaining footage – when they were around the boys tended to be more guarded. I decided to film my reaction to receiving the fateful envelope that would tell me whether I was in the team for the First Test or not. I had scored four tries in five games and thought I must be in with a chance. I could not sleep with excitement the night before so I rose early and waited outside the lift for Samantha Peters, our administrative secretary, who was the bearer of tidings. I filmed the build-up but when I found out I hadn't made it I was crushed. To make matters worse, the letter started 'Congratulations' so I thought I was in until I read the rest of it which told me I was a substitute.

The video does not show how I reacted because I did not turn the camera on again for two days. I was sulking, which was totally out of order. There were 14 players who would not be involved at all – what must the feeling have been like for them? I was bitterly disappointed because I thought I had done enough to make the side but we had discussed back at Weymouth how we would handle that moment when it arrived and I had preached professionalism. When the moment came I did not show it.

Being a substitute is an exhausting experience mentally.

You have to be primed and ready to go throughout a game but may never actually have the chance to release that pent-up energy. I wanted to get on during that momentous First Test in Cape Town but at the same time I did not want to see any of my teammates injured. I had a splitting headache with the stress of it all. Neil Jenkins kept us in the hunt with five penalties but we trailed 16–15 with seven minutes left. Geech had told me he intended to use me as a tactical substitute as the game wore on and when Alan Tait spilled a pass he told me to get ready. But then the game was turned on its head by a cheeky breakaway try from Matt Dawson which contained an outrageous overhead dummy. Taity rounded things off with a last-minute try in the corner and we had won a famous victory.

The fact that it was Taity who scored did not do my chances of playing in the Second Test much good but two incidents the following week changed all that. First, I scored a hat trick against Free State and then the following day Ieuan Evans tore a groin in training and was ruled out of the tour. I was in for the match that would decide the tour. Before the team was announced I went up and commiserated with him that his tour was over. He wished me all the best. It was funny but Ieuan seemed to cheer up at that point, like a big weight had been lifted from his shoulders. His girlfriend flew out and Ieuan stayed with the tour for a while as a supporter which seemed to suit him much better.

It must have been difficult for him with a new baby at home and he is a quiet man anyway but I thought he could have made more of an effort than he did. It was as if he didn't really want to be on the tour. He had been the one person I had struggled to relate to in the party because he had been so miserable. Perhaps it was because we were both competing for the same position but he did not seem keen to know me, or anyone for that matter other than the Welsh boys. He was a bit of an oddball really. The Welsh lads would rib him every day about whether he had his Mexican happy hat on or not.

The only minor disappointment for me in the whole scenario was that it looked as if I had won my place by default. In reality I understood from the management that I would have played anyway.

We all knew how much the Second Test meant. Because of the profile of rugby in South Africa, the British Lions were big news out there but we had little idea of the waves the tour was creating at home. I suppose the countless letters and faxes from back home should have given us a clue. After our final warm-up on the field in Durban with a full house of 52,000 eyeing us and the series within our grasp I remarked to Scott Gibbs that it wasn't a good place to have a bad one. That phrase spread to bars and restaurants throughout the tour. The fear of failure is impossible to banish completely.

The Lions had built up a formidable head of steam by then while South Africa's policy of saving their international players until the Test matches had backfired. Another of their major blunders was not bothering with a specialist goalkicker. Only when Jannie de Beer was called up for the Third Test did they rectify this and by then it was too late. For me it was an education watching Neil Jenkins and Tim Stimpson working in training. They used to stay after each session and put in the hours, honing their techniques with Dave Alred, our kicking coach. I had done some goalkicking for Otley and Leeds but had never achieved anything like the consistency of these two because I had never been taught how to kick.

Jenks won us the series with his 30 points in those first two Tests. He looked so super-cool didn't he? Well, he was anything but in the changing rooms beforehand. He spent an hour and a half before each game throwing up in the toilets. He put so much effort into it I was surprised he wasn't inside out by the time he ran on to the field. The sound of Jenks retching would set me off and I would be sick before the game as well. Still, it takes all sorts.

Every player is different in their approach to a match. Tom Smith, of course, was incredibly quiet. Alan Tait never stopped talking, neither did I – it's a way of burning off nervous energy. Jeremy Guscott would saunter in as if it were a Sunday morning kickaround on the park and have a pleasant massage. Some of the forwards liked to bash each other about to prepare for the pain of what they were about to go through. This was a bit inconvenient for the likes of me if I happened to be passing and found myself pinned against a wall by some big, bad-breathed, hairy forward. I struck up a rapport with one of them – Jeremy Davidson, the Irish lock – and we would say a few words of encouragement to each other before kick-off. I liked to go round the dressing room and shake the hand of each of the players.

The build-up close to kick-off in Durban was very much player-led. The coaches would chip in with the odd comment but generally it was the players who were left to their own devices. In the final minutes before kick-off the coaches, physio, doctor and replacements all left. Then there would be 15 of us pulling each other together for the biggest challenge of our rugby lives. You have to be ready to explode out of the tunnel at kick-off so it was a case of keeping our emotions in check in the build-up otherwise we would have been exhausted when it came to kick-off. We did not have an anthem and when the South African one was played we all instinctively put our arms around each other. It is an intimidating time facing a wall of noise like that. Neil Jenkins was on my right and I pulled his head on to my shoulder and rubbed it paternally. It was a way of saying: 'I will be with you for 80 minutes.' It did not matter which particular Lion it was. At that precise moment we would have done anything for each other. The bond was that strong.

For me that Second Test was a game of two tackles – the one I made to flatten Pieter Rossouw early on and the one I missed to let in Andre Joubert. I am not noted for my big tackling and thumping Pieter from a perfect box-kick by Matt Dawson was very satisfying. In that situation you have the choice of jumping for the ball – which is a lottery – or trying to time the hit just as the opponent catches the ball, which is pretty easy. And I managed that one just about right. Conversely I was badly out of position when I went for Joubert, was fended off and in he went for a try which gave South Africa a 15–9 lead. That was a low moment.

It is important at times like those that nobody gets on your back and that the team raise their game collectively to compensate for an individual lapse. They did. The unflappable Jenks edged us back on level terms and then, of course, Jerry Guscott dropped *that* goal. I was waiting outside him for a pass at the time but it was slow ball and the South African defence was fanned out so he did right. I watched it sail over and could not believe it – we were in front. I didn't have time to celebrate much because the Springboks sprinted up to take the kick-off and it was a case of concentrating the mind on the next job. I did not want to be the one that made the mistake, the one who dropped the ball or missed the tackle on Joubert – again.

They threw everything at us in those last five minutes but

somehow we held out. Henry Honiball chipped over our defence when he should have kept the ball in hand and Jenks won the race to the touchdown with me blocking their runner. Austin Healey raced off to take a quick drop-out and I went ballistic with him. 'I was only joking,' he said but nobody was laughing. Jenks took the drop-kick and put it straight into touch. He had just handed the South Africans a scrum on the 22 in perfect drop-goal position. All our hard work, all the countless tackles might have come to nothing with a flick of Honiball's right boot. It never happened. Didier Mene blew his whistle for the end of the game and that was it – we had become only the third side to win a series in South Africa. Oh happy days.

When that final whistle went I wanted to be everywhere at once. With the players, the management, the supporters at Kings Park, my loved ones back home – even with the people crammed into Cleckheaton Rugby Club going barmy in front of a 14-in television. What a moment. No one can ever take that away from us.

There was only a handful of occasions when all 47 of us went out together. On the day before we flew out to South Africa we had a compulsory bonding drink, to seal the end of an excellent week's preparation and team-building, at The Swan pub in Weymouth. Then after that Second Test we celebrated in style. And it was because of this knees-up that the tour suddenly hit the headlines again for all the wrong reasons two years later.

The drug-taking revelations in the *News of the World* were confused as to where they were supposed to have taken place. The newspaper claimed Lawrence Dallaglio and two other tourists had taken Ecstasy after we had won the series in

Durban and then referred to us waking up in Johannesburg. It must have been some trip. What they were referring to actually happened in Durban. Here is what really went on that night. I went out with the golden oldies – Jerry Guscott, Scott Gibbs and Jason Leonard plus Lawrence. We met up with Sky's Stuart Barnes in what must have been the only bar in South Africa with no interest in rugby. It was a trendy sort of place like you would find in the West End of London – not really my scene at all – and we drank champagne and a few beers to accompany the hot beef sandwiches.

Wherever we went there were hangers-on who wanted to be part of the tour. Out of courtesy we were polite to these people and let them be around us even when we wanted to be alone. As well as the players and Stuart there were two or three other blokes in their late twenties hanging around at this bar. I didn't know them and supposed they were fans. After some time I became aware that these people were smoking – and not tobacco. They were high. It went with the mood of the bar. They kept disappearing outside and then reappearing for some reason.

I knew they had taken drugs and it didn't impress me. They didn't offer me any – if they had I would have told them where to stick them – and as far as I was aware they didn't offer drugs to any of the other players. That was the only occasion on which we came into contact with drugs on the tour.

I was uneasy with the surroundings and pestered the lads to get to a livelier venue where we could really celebrate. I had itchy feet and by 1 a.m. we left. We headed back to downtown Durban and a bar called TJs where we had arranged to meet up with the rest of the team. It was heaving. We mingled in with the supporters and drank the night away. In there was Ian McGeechan and his sobbing wife, getting used to the

171

Lions coach's new crew cut which had been delivered by the bald barber, Keith Wood. It was a forfeit for winning the series. The party went on all night. I returned to my hotel room at 8 a.m. and gave my impression of the dawn chorus, bawling 'TWO–NIL!' out of the window at the hotel block opposite, waking any late sleepers. And that was it.

I was shocked by the drugs story when it came out in May 1999. Having got to know Lawrence well and enjoyed being with him I felt very sorry for him. I couldn't understand why such an articulate, switched-on character had allowed himself to get stitched up like that. How could he have been so naïve?

In my opinion his revelations are unfounded and so cannot tarnish that marvellous Lions tour. The fear is that some people will read the story and jump to the conclusion that we were drugged up to the eyeballs and that's why we won. Utter nonsense. For a start there is no drug culture in rugby and for seconds if anyone was foolish enough to indulge they were liable to be caught. The lads were randomly drugs tested throughout the tour and nobody failed. Players are picked out after each international match to be tested as well. Lawrence was done four times last year.

Giving a urine sample after a game is particularly difficult. Having sweated out fluid, it is a painful business trying to provide enough to satisfy the testers. The procedure is the same in union and league with random numbers drawn out to decide which players have to deliver. The key to it is not blow what little liquid you have at your disposal when you hear the running water of the shower.

I have never encountered a player who uses banned drugs in either of my careers, which made Lawrence's 'revelations' all the more unbelievable. Long may that continue. Nevertheless Lawrence has a lot of work to do to rebuild his reputation. His admissions of drug taking in his youth were never news to other players and they came as a big surprise to me. Personally I have never taken drugs. I've been offered them and been in the company of individuals who have but I have never felt the need to. The approach to drugs is moving on. They used to be a dirty word but society is changing. There are campaigns to legalize soft drugs like cannabis but I do not support them. As a policeman you realize how much crime is caused by people desperate for the money to feed their drugs habit. I've seen a lot of people on drugs and they don't look cool, they look terrible.

The only 'drug' I take is creatine which is legal. I used creatine throughout the tour to enhance my performance but it is more of a health supplement really. It is the equivalent of eating a lot of steaks in a short period of time and while there is some unsubstantiated concern over its long-term effects, there are short-term advantages. The manufacturers claim it helps to sustain a player during high-intensity workouts and speeds up recovery time so he is able to train harder. Whether this is correct or not I don't know but just thinking this might be true has a beneficial effect.

It was a shame Lawrence fell foul of the tabloids because he is a born leader if ever there was one and was a good choice as England captain. The manner in which he plays the game is inspiring to those around him and he is a fine communicator. When he is required to talk he can do and can handle the media. Unfortunately liking the sound of his own voice contributed to his downfall. Much more one of the boys than Will Carling, Lawrence does have a wild side, which I enjoyed sharing with him, but that isn't a crime.

Looking back at the first professional Lions tour there was a surprising amount of drinking. It occurred mainly in small groups but when we went for it we did Britain and Ireland proud. The intensity of the rugby on that tour was huge – the highest I have experienced in either code – so a night out enabled us to let off steam. If the management had banned us we would only have sneaked out of the back door so they were wise to leave us to our own devices. There was never any trouble. After we had lost the third Test, we had a big Saturday night out. It went on late – very late – and I ended up getting to bed at 8 a.m. I tucked myself in with Fran's words ringing around my head that the sponsors Scottish Provident were holding a party next day at noon and that we were all expected to show up. I got up at 1 p.m.

I was badly hungover but managed to get across to The Outback pub in Johannesburg two hours into the function. Everyone was there – the management, the players and the press. It was a free bar and I ordered a pint of lager shandy in an attempt to con everyone that I was having a beer. I felt terrible. That pint sat by me for an hour. The longer I left it the worse it got – in the end I gave it up as a bad job. Whether it was the relaxed atmosphere or Fran declaring the tour officially over, the afternoon slowly moved into a higher gear and we ended up getting on the beer big style.

Players were singing and dancing and laughing and two or three of the lads were due to get married when they went home, so it turned into an impromptu stag party. Barry Williams was one of them – he ended up being stripped down to his underpants and tied to a post outside the pub. I had a wrestling match with Nick Cain from the *Sunday Times*. Even those who did not normally drink, like Tony Underwood and Tom Smith, joined in as we passed round the cup we had won and emptied it of champagne. The revellers ran up a bar bill of £3,000 which takes some doing in a place as cheap as

174

South Africa. For me the evening ended up at the relatively early time of 8 p.m. but by then I was poleaxed, largely from the effects of the previous night.

In hindsight the South Africans should have been raising a glass to us as well. They needed that defeat to bring them down to earth. It's not until you lose that the problems in your game are generally addressed. The arrogance that permeates their rugby was exploded by the defeat to the Lions – after all we were from the northern hemisphere, the second division of world rugby. They thought they were the best and we proved they weren't. So they sat down and changed the plan. The route one approach which they thought would destroy us was adapted to a wider game. Carel du Plessis was discarded and a new coach, Nick Mallett, pressed the right buttons, made a couple of changes and won the Tri-Nations Series in 1998. South Africa went on to equal the world record of consecutive victories with 17 before England finally beat them when they were exhausted at the end of a long southern hemisphere season. I'm sure they would love the chance to play the Lions again now.

For us Lions the profile of the game in South Africa on that trip was a real eye-opener. It was the equivalent of soccer in England. The players were like film stars endorsing products here, there and everywhere. The games drew massive crowds to great stadiums around the country. They were overwhelmingly white but there were a few black faces dotted around. The Lions went to Soweto to help with a training camp there but I couldn't go because I was preparing for a game, which was a shame because I would have liked to have seen it. We were only exposed to this other side of South Africa in passing. It was so sad to see the conditions that some people had to live in. I was amazed to see the shanty towns on the way back to the airport after we had played in Bloemfontein. There were streams of people walking back to their shacks after work to a life we could not even imagine. This in a country as wealthy as South Africa. And the threat of violence was constant. Everywhere we went we were warned to be vigilant by the local liaison officers who told us the no-go zones. Wherever we parked there seemed to be people with sticks guarding cars. It is a country of contrasts, beautiful but dangerous.

It would have been wonderful to have gone to Robben Island to see what Nelson Mandela had to put up with in his years in prison, just as it would have been to go on a safari or visit Sun City. But we went as a professional sporting team and we had a job to do. Being tourists and explorers came second. Some day I would love to go back to see it all again and even to play there once more. All our matches were televised live and I hope the tour helped to spread the gospel amongst South Africa's black population. There are some tremendous athletes amongst them and if they get hooked on rugby the Springboks will be even better. Mind you, rugby is made for the Afrikaners. They are big, strong and powerful, and relish the physical contact. They also don't mind playing it dirty.

While the Springboks learned from their defeat, I don't think British and Irish rugby built on the success as much as it could and should have done. The players returned bright-eyed to their clubs, dead set on taking the game forward over here by playing the Lions style. It never happened – the pressure to produce success at their clubs was too great. It was silly really: we had just beaten the world champions with that style and for once put the northern hemisphere ahead of the southern hemisphere but not many clubs dared risk it.

However it's probably true that if we had played a little less open stuff in the Third Test we might have whitewashed the Springboks. We were a bit dumb on occasions during that game. But in many ways that was probably a better game to watch for the neutral than the first two internationals. In Tests the pressure tends to make players withdraw into themselves and not elaborate or take chances so the spectacle is not always so good. But with the series decided the football we played in the Third Test meant I enjoyed it more than the second. It meant I was able to get the ball in my hands more often. Missing out on a 3–0 victory was a shame, not least because Fran Cotton would have lost his hair like Geech if we had managed a whitewash. Although that would have needed the presence of someone brave enough to tie him down first.

The type of rugby we were playing outside the Tests was wonderful. It was similar to what you would see in the Super-12 series. The game against Free State when we won 52–30 contained the best rugby I have ever been involved in. Relentless phases of possession allowed us to carve out some scintillating scores, ripping a very useful side apart. I don't think the South Africans could believe they were seeing that quality of open rugby from us.

The Free State game wasn't great for everyone though. Will Greenwood lost his lucky blue trunks after the game which was probably not a bad thing considering the amount of good fortune they brought him that day. He almost died on the pitch after being knocked out cold in a tackle. At one point it looked like he wasn't going to come round at all and even our doctor James Robson was a worried man. So much for the lucky trunks.

It is surprising how many seemingly intelligent and

balanced rugby players are superstitious. I claim not to be but I always run out third, bang the ball three times on each shoulder and strap my left ankle and wrist before my right. It is a routine and if I have a poor game I look to see if I have done anything different in the build-up. If I have I will endeavour not to do it again and then everything will work out fine next time. Won't it? It's a bit silly really.

The Lions tour turned my life upside-down but hopefully it did not change me. A year before if I'd have turned up at Bath nobody would have recognized me. Post-South Africa, we were all big news. I appeared on daytime television having a makeover – I think the makers of *Turnstyle* must have mixed me up with Jerry Guscott. Then there was *Live and Dangerous*, Channel 5's late-night show with Dominik Diamond. The transmission only started at midnight so I presumed it must be an adult fantasy channel and turned up in my leopardskin underpants. There was Michael Parkinson's Radio 5 show with Angus Fraser and Barry Hearn and numerous requests from newspapers and Sky. I appeared on a radio show hosted by Will Carling which was the first time I had spoken to him since I clouted him in my early union days. There were no hard feelings. It was the first programme he had done in his new career so I told him I'd take over if he was struggling.

Fame came late for me at 30 but that was a good thing. The likes of Jonny Wilkinson, thrust into the limelight at 18 when he made his England debut, can find the glare of the media daunting. Older, though not necessarily wiser, I lapped it up. I enjoy an opportunity to express my feelings and my opinions. I get emotional talking about the tour when I realize how much it meant to people. Sometimes I pop the video on to bring back the memories. I should be at peace with myself over it all but there is a lot of sorrow in me that it has gone and I can never repeat the camaraderie of those seven weeks.

Geech said in one of his team talks about how, in years to come, we would see each other and know with just one look the special something being a Lion had given to us. He was right. We had a reunion dinner in London after we returned and whenever I have met any of those Lions since, there has been an extra firmness in the handshake or warmth in the hug. They were seven weeks that changed all of our lives.

Chapter 10

Jack Rowell is an interesting character. He coached England to a lot of success including making the 1995 World Cup semi-final, yet even after going through all that with him I don't think many of the players could say they really understood him. Not many of the players liked him and he had the reputation of being a law unto himself. So when I headed out to Australia for my England recall in 1997 nine years on from my first cap Jason Leonard and Jerry Guscott joked that they would have paid their own fares to have eavesdropped at the initial meeting between myself and Jack.

Rowell left me out of the original squad to play Australia in the one-off Test in Sydney at the end of the Lions tour but told me later he only did it to be contrary. The night before the England line-up was revealed I had scored *that* try against Gauteng at Ellis Park and Jack said he had it in his mind to pick me but that he decided not to because everyone would have expected him to after the try. His intention was always to add me to the squad the following week. Which he did.

Jack held a welcome meeting for the Lions boys who were joining up with the England team that had just drawn the series 1–1 in Argentina. He gave a special mention to Matt Dawson, who had risen from England's No. 4 scrum-half to No. 1 in the space of a few weeks, and to myself who, he said, had come from 'another world'. Privately he added the two of us would meet again so he could get to know me. The days ticked by and still there was no word from Jack. Then, on the morning of the Test, his assistant Les Cusworth came to my room to tell me I had been summoned. We had a chat for three-quarters of an hour about him, me, England, the Lions and life in general. To be honest I think we both felt a bit let down by what we found. We got on extremely well and there were no explosions. But I was totally baffled by his timing. I like to use the hours leading up to a game to concentrate on the match itself not on making friends.

I was very disappointed with the atmosphere in the England camp. Everybody was tired after a long season and summer tour and people said it was a game too far but that should never be the case when players pull on an England shirt. I had an extra spring in my step because it was just like a first cap for me. Nevertheless I felt strange having been an influential figure on the Lions tour and suddenly arriving in this very different environment. I expected to be quiet as the new boy but so was everyone else. It was all very low key. Phil de Glanville, who was the captain, was laid-back and easy going but that did not help in providing leadership. In fact there was none. It came to the day before the game and I realized I had to become more involved and have an input otherwise we could have been in for a hiding. So I did.

We lost and played poorly but the thrashing never arrived. Phil's lack of presence was demonstrated during the game when we conceded a try and gathered together in a huddle. This is the time when an inspiring captain can make a real difference to a team but Phil hardly said anything. His missed tackle had led to the try and I think he found it difficult to pull everyone together when we all realized he was the weak link. A captain has to be worth his place in a team and Phil, good player though he was, failed to make the grade.

Jack Rowell was replaced as coach after that match but in a way he had already gone. I invited him over for a drink with the lads after the game and he joined us. I could tell it was Jack's swansong. He had been treated shabbily by the Rugby Football Union who had been tapping up possible successors behind his back and I'm sure he knew his time was up. The RFU wanted someone who would pander to them but Jack wasn't one of them. He was very much his own man, opinionated and not one to bow down to anyone.

The Clive Woodward regime was completely different. It was like a breath of fresh air – everything was positive and businesslike. He had been a flamboyant player and some of his ideas were very exciting too although others were a bit mystifying. He was a big fan of the way the Lions had brought the game on and of what was happening in the Super-12s as well as rugby league. The problem was he couldn't coach what he preached. There was Clive, England A coach Richard Hill and John Mitchell trying to introduce certain rugby league moves but, to be honest, they did not know what they were talking about, having never done them as players themselves. They were moves they had either picked up from a rugby league coaching manual or from the television. Clive was teaching them all wrong and I felt embarrassed for him. There was one called a flash whereby a player switches to the blind side at pace and takes a pass to create a three-on-two overlap which just was not working. I had a word to explain what should have been happening but I had to tread on eggshells because I had only just got back into the fold. The last thing I wanted was another period in exile.

It needed the involvement of a specialist from league like Phil Larder to enable things to work. England had already recognized the value of rugby league expertize. Les Cusworth, a big fan of league, had been to see Dean Bell at Leeds and Brian Smith, the ex-Bradford Bulls coach, out in Australia to watch the way they worked and to pinch some ideas. I admired what Clive was trying to do but I think he was guilty of trying to make England run before they could walk. The open style is all very well but England do not have the personnel to play it. Clive, rightly, believes that if a player is representing his country he should be able to catch, pass and recognize an overlap. The Lions chose to use two props in Tom Smith and Paul Wallace who could just about hold their own in the scrums but who were explosive runners with the ball in hand. England do not have that type of player. Jason Leonard and Darren Garforth do what they do very well but they are not all-round footballers.

After the 1997 Lions tour and the England comeback in Australia that followed, I was reacquainted with rugby league. I rejoined a Halifax team which had lost their last 11 matches and was about to face Canterbury, Canberra and Brisbane. They were three of the stronger Australian sides in the ill-fated World Club Championship which only lasted one season because of the endless mismatches. It wouldn't have mattered if it had been the weaker ones – they were still too good for the English clubs even with a contrived qualification process for the knockout stages which bent over backwards to help our sides. Physically, I felt just about OK but mentally I was shattered. The Lions tour was a massive high and I don't think I realized how much it took out of me at the time. A lot of players lost form the season afterwards and I was one of them. Only for me, with my dual code commitments, it happened instantly.

Halifax told me they wanted me to play against Canberra and I felt duty-bound to do so. We suffered the inevitable defeat and then it was Brisbane. Sky were covering the game live and during it I sprung a rib cartilage. As I was stretchered off I'm sure a lot of people must have been thought I was faking in order to have some time off. If only. That injury kept me out for the next three months and effectively plunged my career into a downward spiral. I was in a lot of pain when it happened as the muscle went into spasm and I overheard one of the St John's Ambulancemen telling his colleague I might have punctured a lung. That sent me into a worse spasm. The pain would not go away even when I returned to Newcastle in September and eventually it came to the point where Rob Andrew told me I had to play. To be honest I think he thought I was swinging the lead at Newcastle. But I wasn't – the injury would not go away. It was probably my body's way of telling me I needed a rest after four years of continuous rugby.

If I had taken a blow in the rib area I would have been in agony so I was timid at first but ended up playing three games in a week and scoring a hat trick in the first one against Edinburgh in the European Conference. We lost in Biarritz though and I was made a scapegoat and dropped. I don't know why. There were others who performed far worse that day. For once our forwards were outplayed but time and again we kept switching back inside. Suddenly in the last 10 minutes the backs were expected to win a game where they had not been allowed to make a contribution to the opening

70 minutes. I spoke to Rob about it at the airport before we flew home but the roof really fell in when Sir John blew his top with our management team.

Under pressure from above they felt they had to take action. Newcastle regarded me as an individual who was too unpredictable to fit into the team pattern. Where once that was a plus, now they didn't like it. I was left out of the team on a regular basis and the travelling up the A1 became a drag. A four-hour round-trip is a long way to go to hold a tackle bag. On one occasion one of the other wingers got injured in training and they looked around for me to slot in but as I hadn't been named in the original side I had already left.

Looking back, being dropped for the penultimate game of the previous season against Waterloo was probably the first sign that all was not well between me and the club. I had made a couple of errors in a couple of games but no one had mentioned a thing until I got the chop. I phoned Rob in a temper and said I expected him of all people to be able to communicate with his players. His efforts at it had been appalling on this occasion. He hadn't much to say in response. I came on as a substitute during that game but my confidence had taken such a jolt that when a glaring hole appeared on the outside I did not dare go for it and came back inside. Steve Bates, who along with Rob and Dean Ryan ran the show at Newcastle, then told me they hadn't been happy with me for a couple of weeks. I couldn't weigh Bates up. As I mentioned he did not think I was good enough to be a Lion and he told one player that while I might have known a lot about rugby league I knew nothing about rugby union.

My relationship with Rob deteriorated as I was left out of the side the following season which was a shame because we had been pretty close at first. Sandy and I had dined at Rob's house and he was always checking to see how the family was. But I was disappointed in his man management which I thought would have been his strength. Eighty per cent of the coach's job is man management as far as I am concerned – it's so important to be able to treat people as individuals rather than as a herd, which is what happened at Newcastle. Whenever there was a one-on-one problem I felt that he shied away from it and chose not to address the issue.

I deliberately tried not to become a burden – I had seen the effect moaning, disgruntled players had on squads before – but I was desperately unhappy. A lot of my teammates could not believe why I was not in the side and rang me to find out why. They presumed it must have been something personal. I tell people it's because I slept with Rob's wife – which isn't true.

At the root of the problem was something which stemmed from the Lions tour. Rob said he wanted to rest the Lions players periodically to stop them being burned out after playing over the summer. Which was fine except a considerable part of my wages was determined by appearance fees. I asked Rob if we could restructure the payments so I would receive a smaller percentage of my money as a match fee. He agreed and came back with an offer. I expected to lose out a little under the new arrangements but the figure he produced was quite a lot less. He said it had come from the board and was non-negotiable. I had to take it or leave it.

Being injured I was watching a match with Ken Nottage, the general manager, when he brought up the subject. He asked if I was happy with the proposal and I told him it fell short of what I was after. Then he said it was only the club's initial offer and he expected me to come back with one of my own for us to negotiate. Clearly there had been a misunderstanding and I confronted Rob about it. It was a big mistake as far as our relationship was concerned – Rob thought I had gone behind his back. In the end I settled for the deal Rob had offered me but things were never the same between us.

I have to take my share of the blame for what happened. I was rolling along on the top of a wave after the summer and maybe my mind wasn't totally on the job. Nevertheless it was very frustrating to hear Newcastle talk about playing the Lions style of game and end up never receiving the ball. Rob had been out there watching and he said we would be adopting an expansive game but it never happened. An extraordinary tactical decision he made summed things up. He decided the team could not pass as well off their left hands as their right so the right winger – me – was never to receive the ball from first-phase possession. Someone had to be used as a battering ram in midfield first. This cut the number of passes I would receive down to an absolute minimum. I understand entirely the business of conforming to the team pattern but I felt this was taking things too far. When I'm stood out on the right wing and there is no one in front of me I should get the ball, regardless of what the plan is.

The business about not passing well off our left hands seemed ridiculous to me. I couldn't believe what I was hearing. If Rob couldn't do it, he should have stayed out on the field and practised it rather than basing our game around his weaknesses. In my view, Rob's passing under pressure was not as strong as it could be and he was simply unable to stand flat to the opposition ranks and put a man through a gap. If we had a lineout on our own 22, he could never conceive of running the ball out. I think that's where a side is at its most dangerous, when it can do the unexpected. The only way to score a try is with the ball in your hands not with it up in the stands. I came to realize that our philosophies were miles apart.

I tried to help in training, adding my experience much as I did on the Lions tour but my contribution wasn't welcomed. We had one move called a dummy scissor pop where I was expected to appear outside Inga and take a pop pass. Steve wanted me to take the ball deep which, as far as I was concerned, was all wrong. I had to take it shallow to have any chance of the move working. I was very frustrated but while Inga and Alan Tait privately thought similarly their view was that Newcastle were paying our wages so we should just keep quiet and do what we were told. That wasn't my style and it rubbed up Bates the wrong way. He, Dean and Rob ran an extremely tight ship, too tight in my opinion. It was like a master/slave relationship. Do as they say or else you're out. We used to receive bollockings like schoolchildren if we played badly.

Yet Newcastle blew the established order wide open in their first season in the top flight and won the league. Why? Simple. They were a great side. The forwards were immense and the backs pretty good when they were allowed to play. They may have been boring and predictable but it was effective rugby. The comparison with the football club across the city was apt. Kevin Keegan may have put together a wonderfully exciting side but what did they win? In time clubs always catch up with a power game – it happened to Newcastle just the same as it happened in rugby league to Bradford Bulls – but in the 1997–8 season the Falcons deserved to win the thrilling Allied Dunbar Premiership title race with Saracens. It was just a shame I couldn't be there with them.

Being left out at Newcastle was all the worse because it cost me my place in the England side. I was in line to play against Australia in the first of the four pre-Christmas internationals but Clive Woodward, the new coach, told me I needed to be playing first-team rugby. I had Clive in one ear saying I needed to play and Rob in the other saying he wasn't going to pick me. He obviously thought Graham Childs was a better player. Fortunately Clive did not and he gave me another route in with the midweek games against the awesome All Blacks. I wished he hadn't after the Emerging England match at Huddersfield. First of all I was up against Jonah Lomu and secondly the rest of his teammates were on fire. We were slaughtered and I had a shocker.

I knew I had to impress and I tried to play to my strengths by running the ball out of defence as often as I could. Good idea, wrong opposition. Every time I did I was hit by this black wall and possession was turned over. We were outclassed. And Jonah was massive – he should be made to play in the forwards. If he ever gets back to his best, the world had better watch out. Even on three-quarter throttle he is awesome. Afterwards he came over and sat with me and we spoke at length about our respective careers and the kidney condition which threatened his career and which he still lives with. He surprised me with what a nice bloke he was. I expected him to be arrogant like some of the All Blacks can be but he wasn't at all. I'm sure the illness put everything into perspective for him.

The next week Jonah was on the sidelines and we had a real go at the tourists in the guise of the English Rugby

Partnership XV at Bristol and almost beat them. I had a good game and was called up to join the England squad for the third of the autumn internationals against South Africa. I thought it would be a case of holding the tackle shields for the first team but Clive informed me when I arrived at training that I was taking Adedayo Adebayo's place. I was as chuffed as chuffed could be. It was one of my unfulfilled dreams to play in an international at Twickenham.

I made sure I soaked up every moment of it. I took special care to enjoy the build-up, the crowd and the atmosphere. It was a wonderful occasion with a full house there to see us take on the world champions. Running out at Twickenham was a tremendous experience. One minute you are squeezed into the surprisingly short tunnel, the next you are out of it and straight on to the grass to be met by a wall of noise. Even though the pitch is so big the stands are so tall that there is a feeling of claustrophobia. As a player it is a wonderful place to play but having sat in the crowd at Twickenham a few times I have been disappointed with the atmosphere. There are a lot of corporate types present who have never been to rugby matches before and they just sit back and wait to be entertained rather than be proactive and get behind their team. You only had to look at what happened when England took a game to Old Trafford in 1997 to see what the support could be like. That day northern rugby union fans really got behind their side, so much so that the players did a lap of honour in appreciation even though they had lost to New Zealand.

The game itself against South Africa was a let-down. Unfortunately I didn't have much of an opportunity to make an impact and every time I went looking for work the ball seemed to shoot off in the opposite direction. We lost and I was substituted which was a bit embarrassing. When I saw the No. 14 being waved about on the touchline I thought it was the signal for their winger to come off. I was surprised it was me because we were only a score behind at the time, a situation made for me to produce something. But they were demanding opposition and perhaps in hindsight I was off the pace with my disjointed preparation – Clive reiterated afterwards the need for me to be playing first-team football. Unfortunately the next time I had a run of first-team games was four months later on loan at Rotherham, where I played pretty badly. Not quite what either of us had in mind.

I don't hold any grudges against Clive even though he effectively ended my international career. I still feel a sense of underachievement in not having played in the Five Nations Championship. I would have loved to have performed in that competition. Even playing the world champions, South Africa, I felt as if there was something missing. There is no substitute for tradition and rivalry. Some may say that putting Italy into the tournament spoils it but the same people would have kept the game amateur. I think it is a positive move which will bring more revenue in and help to make a magnificent tournament even more successful.

England missed out on the Five Nations title in Clive's first two seasons but, whatever his shortcomings, one thing you could not accuse him of was shying away from youth. Sometimes it didn't work, as in the case of Bath hooker Andy Long, who was substituted after half a game against Australia, but sometimes it did. Step forward Jonny Wilkinson.

Newcastle bought a team of ready-made stars but they also realized they had to look to the future by bringing in some youngsters. It is always a bit of a gamble when you are earmarking young players for great things because they can change an awful lot in a short period of time. Some make the step up from being schoolboy wonders, others don't. Many factors can play their part – injury, physical development, mental attitude and luck as well. Newcastle cannot have known when they brought in an unknown kid called Jonny Wilkinson just what gold dust they had in their grasp, but from my first sight of him in the development team I could see he oozed class. The way he handled the ball showed that he was destined to be a very good player – nothing was forced, everything came naturally. He also handled himself well and was very mature for his age. Where a lot of 18-year-olds with his talent would have been cocky, he was quiet, not too full of himself and he was willing to listen. Rob was his mentor, doing a lot of kicking with him and obviously viewing him as his heir apparent.

I was asked by a publishing company who were moving into rugby for the names of some up-and-coming stars and the one I mentioned was Jonny Wilkinson. On the same day he was included in the England squad for the first time. You only had to watch him in training to see his potential. He had an aura around him which is rare in one so young. You don't get talent like that very often. Rugby has a knack of sorting out average players and he has just risen above the pack.

Woodward recognized his talent and backed his own judgment. It didn't work out at first when Jonny drowned at stand-off in a weak England team on the southern hemisphere tour in 1998 but when he was recalled to the first-choice team he flowered. Initially he was the victim of a syndrome that affects a lot of promising youngsters – they are only given a chance as a last option. But now he has been given a proper opportunity and he is taking it superbly. It is very rare for a youngster to be put into a strong side and he must make the most of it. I was surprised when he was picked at centre by England – he is a stand-off through and through – but the strength of his tackling carried him out of trouble. It is tremendous for a player of his size.

He has all the skill but he has to harness that with experience and in a way the timing of Rob Andrew's injury at the end of the 1998–9 season was perfect. It gave Jonny a chance to show what he could do in the position he will eventually play. Rob had sheltered Jonny well but that had its disadvantage because it denied him the chance to learn. Performing regularly at No. 10 for Newcastle is vital to his development. Once this is secure what England need to do is to tell Jonny he has the stand-off spot for a fixed period and let him grow into the job. That way he will become England's stand-off for the foreseeable future. He will undoubtedly be targeted and if the opposition forwards get him at the bottom of a ruck he will come out pretty sore, but he's a tough cookie. Newcastle have expanded their style – and not before time – which will give Jonny the chance to bring on his game. He has to be given the freedom to play attacking rugby because he is so naturally talented. It would be a criminal waste of talent if all of his skills weren't employed to the full.

Jonny and England have no excuses with regards to preparation. In my experience the back-up the Rugby Football Union provided to the England team was superb. Nothing was left to chance. Everything was structured, team talks were like sales meetings. Whatever Clive Woodward needed, Clive Woodward got. The difference with league where international football is almost an afterthought was massive. Woodward has been helped by the thawing in relations between the clubs and the Union – the ongoing row between the two was a major threat to England's success. At the height of it we were told by Newcastle that under no circumstances were we to do contact work with England in our one-day midweek training sessions in case we returned with an injury. We ignored that directive. The frosty relationship between the clubs and the RFU took a long time to improve but after threats of players being withdrawn from England tours they eventually came to a truce that enabled the national side to have a clear run at the 1999 World Cup unhindered by club distractions. It had to make sense. Nothing will stimulate interest in Premiership rugby more than success by England. But all is not sweetness and light yet.

There is still some spilt milk to cry over before we have stability. Even with the salary cap in operation, the ambitions of some clubs will push them beyond their means. Like Rotherham. Their efforts in reaching the Second Division play-offs two seasons running were unbelievable but my advice to any player considering joining this most upwardly mobile of clubs, which came from nowhere to the brink of the top flight, is simple: Don't.

One of the reasons for playing my loan stint at Rotherham was that there was a promise of a three-year contract waiting at the end of it which would be worth £225,000 to me. But when I tried to finalize the arrangement things started to unravel. When I finally managed to pin the management down I was told that the deal was off. I was appalled. If the club had admitted they were having problems meeting the terms I would have been more sympathetic. It was a massive amount of money for Rotherham, who were living beyond their means in an attempt to reach the top flight. Even without my wages they had to draw up a Creditors Voluntary Agreement the following season because of financial problems. I got a mention on the list of creditors but it said I was owed nothing.

Remember this was the club I had helped out by insisting Halifax and Newcastle make good on the verbal agreement I had with Rotherham. I am the first to admit that my performances at Rotherham were not what they should have been, although their style of play did not particularly suit me. But what made their about-turn even more galling was that it cost me a place at Leicester, who went on to become the Premiership champions that season. When I eventually found out that Rotherham had changed their minds I contacted Dean Richards, the Leicester manager, who told me he would have signed me if he had known about my availability six weeks earlier but that he had now sorted out his squad.

Rotherham's mismanagement was symptomatic of that affecting rugby union at large as the bubble of professionalism began to burst. The whole catalogue of financial disasters and forced mergers that befell the sport began when the RFU failed to sign up the top players to the Union, as had the southern hemisphere nations. Clubs dived in with offers to players which proved unsustainable and it was those players who suffered when the sport came down to earth. It is hard for someone to accept being paid less for the same job once they have become accustomed to a certain income. If they still had a job: there were plenty of others at the end of the 1998–9 season without anything. Squads were being trimmed back and some clubs were forced to merge to try to balance the books and all because the game had got the numbers wrong in the first place. How the sport could simply lose Richmond and London Scottish, two of its most famous names, was criminal.

Perhaps it was asking too much of rugby union to get professionalism right at the first attempt – rugby league still gets it wrong after more than 100 years – but it wasn't the players' fault that somebody could not do their sums properly. The gravy train had to stop somewhere but for players who had sacrificed other careers and made commitments, naïvely believing what was written on their contracts, the return to the real world has provided a bitter pill to swallow. And it wasn't only in union that the figures weren't adding up.

The £87m Sky had promised for rugby league had been downgraded to £56.8m over five years once the Super League war had been sorted out and that reduction left a big hole in the accounts. The game wasn't such a valuable pawn in the TV war any more and, as Sky had rugby league where it wanted it, the sport simply had to accept the pay cut. Rugby league must have been the only sport to have negotiated a reduction in TV income in recent years. With this handicap clubs, again, were finding their income did not match their expenditure and players had to be sacrificed. I was one of them.

The end, when it came, at Halifax in the summer of 1998 was amicable but tinged with disappointment for me. I had returned from rugby union wanting to have a real blast at rugby league. Mentally, I was revved up and raring to go but physically those years of back-to-back rugby had taken their toll. The injuries I had played through and shrugged off in the past suddenly became serious enough to keep me off the field for long periods. When this happens you start to question why.

I injured my knee ligaments in my first game back at Halifax and no sooner had I returned than I dislocated my foot in our 'on the road' game at Northampton. These were matches designed to spread the gospel of Super League and turned out to be a qualified success – except for me.

To make matters worse for the first time in my career I found myself at a club which was not paying its players on time. It was a period of upheaval for the Blue Sox who had moved in with their soccer neighbours Halifax Town at The Shay. Thrum Hall was a very intimidating place to play for opponents. The ground was 10ft higher on one side of the pitch than the other which made for a big advantage to the home side and when it was full there was a cracking atmosphere. But under the terms of the 'Framing The Future' document, which was supposed to point the way ahead for clubs, grounds had to be improved and if you had thrown £500,000 at dilapidated Thrum Hall no one would have noticed the difference. The problem for Halifax was nobody wanted to buy the place. It took a while for The Shay to feel like home, particularly as we continued to train at Thrum Hall but the theory was that one day it would be upgraded into a modern stadium.

So much for the long term. Staring us in the face was an obvious cash-flow problem which was to end up with the club staving off a winding-up order. As players we were having to scrabble around for the money that was rightfully ours. These financial problems contributed to the club's decision to let me go, although it was the spate of injuries that was officially blamed. I had been around long enough to understand where they were coming from but it was still a wrench after six largely happy years.

So where next? With the 1998–9 union season coming up, Harlequins expressed an interest in taking me. They were talking about a three-month contract but they were struggling at the time and in the end I decided it would have been too much of a risk to move to London and away from my family on such a short-term arrangement.

At the back of my mind was also the wear and tear that year-round rugby was taking. I still wanted to play top-class rugby but a winter off was appealing. My decision was made for me when Malcolm Reilly was appointed coach at Huddersfield Giants. Reilly had been a great influence on my career and a third spell together was something we both fancied. Besides Huddersfield could only improve on the previous season when they won just two games. Couldn't they?

The Malcolm Reilly I discovered had changed after his experiences Down Under where he had been a success in charge of Newcastle Knights. He had mellowed a lot. Malcolm's legendary temper had been brought under control to the point where he would never blow his top after a match but save up for a more rational inquisition the day after. But he allowed people like Paul Loughlin to get away with murder in training. The words 'comfort zone' were invented for Paul. Reilly had brought back new ideas from Australia and while he was no longer 10 years ahead of his time, as he'd been during his early days as a coach, he was still looking to push back the boundaries.

He was more into mental rehearsal and goal setting and he was also more keen to involve the players themselves in the analysis. Before each game we had to write down and hand in our own views on opposition strengths and weaknesses. Then after each one we had to write down what we had done wrong and right. One column tended to be a lot more full than the other. What Reilly probably found frustrating though was working with players inferior to the ones he had been used to Down Under. The quality players simply weren't available to sign over here and the ones Huddersfield were stuck with made the sort of basic errors that would have driven a lesser coach mad.

A lot of the younger players did not know Malcolm and were intimidated by his presence and reputation. When we went on a pre-season jolly to Malaga, where it rained more heavily than in Yorkshire, we embarked on a mammoth two-day drinking binge and encountered a sober Reilly in a bar at the end of the night. The younger boys were terrified and put up a pitiful attempt at being coherent to try to impress him. I knew him better than that. After all he was the man who taught me vitally important rugby lessons like being careful who you stood next to in the shower. If it was Malcolm you were likely to experience a different coloured shower running down your leg. Apparently it sorts out your athlete's foot a treat.

Huddersfield were bankrolled by a local millionaire called Ken Davy. He used to come into the dressing room before kick-off to wish us luck and you would rarely see him without a smile on his face. But I have to question what he was up to, pouring his money down the drain at Huddersfield. He didn't know much about rugby – he just wanted his hometown team to do well, I suppose. One thing is for certain, they were very lucky to have him.

Ken would have been better off diverting some of his fortune into a marketing operation for the Giants. Where the likes of Bradford had more people promoting the club than playing the game, Huddersfield had a skeleton staff. They should have been using their players to go into local schools and start the kids talking about the club – I was never once asked to do this sort of basic promotional work.

The magnificent McAlpine Stadium was a façade in many

ways for Huddersfield. It may be a beautifully designed ground which has deservedly won architectural awards but there was one problem – the Giants weren't allowed to train there. The fear of damaging a playing surface also used by Huddersfield Town Football Club meant the rugby players had to prepare at pretty abysmal facilities elsewhere. How can a ground feel like home if you aren't allowed to tread on it. In many ways the McAlpine is too good. Visiting teams loved coming to play there because of the pristine facilities. They didn't have to put up with a vociferous home crowd because there wasn't one – or at least there didn't appear to be because the stands were too large for the number of supporters rugby league attracts. When photographers hand out snaps of tries from Huddersfield games the players are reluctant to take them because the background is always row upon row of empty seats. If people aren't willing to pay to watch, the club have to look at giving free tickets away because a big, partisan crowd can be worth six or seven points to a team. When the Sky cameras came in June for the match against London Broncos it was just embarrassing. An attendance of 2,500 in a ground built for 10 times that looks awful. To make matters worse Glen Air dropped a goal two minutes from time to beat us by a point after I'd had two tries disallowed for being offside from kicks. It was symptomatic of how things were going for the club at the time.

My presence helped to up the level of professionalism at a club which lagged behind other Super League sides. But things weren't happening for me on the field. I questioned myself a lot in the summer of 1999. I have always been very honest with myself but I was left asking myself whether I was still up to it because of my performances. I was in a side that was struggling but I wasn't doing anything in matches. The harder I tried the worse it got. In training I was still ahead of a lot of the younger players. But in matches? Nothing. I have always played at clubs where I have been a hero to supporters but at Huddersfield I copped some flak and I found that hard to deal with. I have always met a challenge head on but this time I was left thinking was it worth it?

Rugby league was increasingly a young man's sport and a lot of my contemporaries had retired. Maybe I should have done the same. Sandy said she did not want to see me working my way down through the Batleys and Bramleys as a sad shadow of the player I used to be. Perhaps my time was up. But was 32 too old? Inside I knew I had something left to offer. Midway through the season just when I thought I was turning the corner, Huddersfield dropped me. And they ended a 10-match losing run by beating Sheffield the next game. That said it all.

The move to Huddersfield, depressing though it was at times, at least gave me the opportunity to renew acquaintances with Bobbie Goulding. That was always liable to be interesting. We are very similar characters – fiery, opinionated and not keen on coming second – so we get on well usually but we are also prone to the odd head to head. We hadn't been at Huddersfield long when we were arguing in the dressing room because Bobbie was blaming my side of the defence for our problems. I let him have a couple of barrels'-worth in return which was billed as a full-scale argument by some of our teammates who obviously did not know us that well. One grumpy training session later we were back to being best mates again. He was a great asset for Huddersfield with his excellent kicking game – a source of more and more tries in rugby league. But even with Bobbie firing the Giants were never going to rip up many trees. Historically they have a wonderful opportunity because the sport was born in the town but fans are only interested in success and Huddersfield have some way to go yet on that score. Their profile is illustrated by the number of people who came up to me at speaking engagements and asked where I had gone. One of the rugby union magazines awarded me 'disappearing act of the year' which I couldn't help laughing at. It was true.

Chapter 11

If I could have a dream testimonial, it would be to field Bentley's All Stars against the best rugby union and rugby league have to offer. My line-up would consist of former rugby league players who have returned to union, and I'd pit them against both codes in two challenge matches, one played under league rules, the other union. Now that would be worth watching. Scott Gibbs and Allan Bateman, Scott Quinnell and Inga Tuigamala ... a tasty proposition in either code. Of course it could never happen – there are countless contractual hurdles that my promise of limitless beer and a mucky woman for the night might not be sufficient to overcome. But then again people said the same about the Bath v. Wigan matches and they went ahead. What made these cross-code games so interesting was that they provided answers to questions that had not been asked before. It was fantasy rugby come to life.

Nothing stirs more bar-room controversy than debating which union players would make it at league and, more relevantly these days, vice versa. For a variety of social and geographical reasons there are many players who have never had the chance to experience both games. I'm sure they would enjoy them. After a lot of thought I've come up with a team of rugby league players to play rugby union and a team of union players to play league, few of whom have experienced the pleasures of the other code. The top players from one are not necessarily the ones I have picked for the other. There's not much point asking Jason Leonard to play league where his set-piece skills are obsolete, just as it is hopeless asking most of the league forwards to play in a union pack because they are too small and unable to adapt to the specialist skills involved.

Having played in both codes at a high level I believe the only aspects they have in common is an oval ball and an aim of scoring tries and goals. They are completely different. Bath v. Wigan proved this. I commentated on the league game at Maine Road for Radio 5 Live and it unfolded exactly as I expected. Bath's backs had a chance but the forwards struggled badly – it was too hard for them to keep up with the pace. Wigan fared better at Twickenham but if Bath had wanted to run up an equally large win they could have just stuck the ball up their jumpers and their opponents would never have seen it. If they repeated the challenge now I think Bath would be closer to Wigan at league because they are all full-time professionals and fitter because of it but they would still be thrashed.

Rugby union has its set disciplines like the scrummage and the lineout which people are bred and nurtured to perform. Accordingly the players are different shapes and sizes. A rugby league team is much harder to pigeonhole because of the way the game has developed. A winger and a prop are virtually interchangeable. It requires powerful ball-handlers from No. 1 to No. 13 and is much more of a game to suit the individual. If you go off and do your own thing, it does not matter if you are tackled behind the gain line because play stops and your team has five more chances. In union if you isolate yourself, the opposition is going to turn over possession so you must conform to the team pattern. This was the main problem for Robbie and Henry Paul when they had short stints in union with Harlequins and Bath respectively. Martin Offiah was a big flop when he joined Bedford too because his individual flair and opportunism were not always beneficial to the team. Once they have appreciated this difference a lot of the leading rugby league backs would be able to swap over to union.

Bearing in mind the difficulties of asking a league player to fill a front five position in union I have had to cheat and select props who are back in union in drawing up my team of league players to take on the world at the 15-man game. Otherwise we could have had a serious accident in the front row. I have also worked on the current limit of four overseas players in the side which is just as well or the whole side might have been Australian!

League XV

Full-back – Kris Radlinski
Good young attacking player who interested the Rugby Football Union until they realized how much it would have cost them. Full-back is an important point of attack in union now – he has the most space to use on the pitch and Radlinski would use it wisely as well as being safe under the high ball.

Right wing – Jason Robinson
A freak. Jumps around like a kangaroo. Can step off either foot and has a decent defence too. A nightmare to defend

207

against and even though he would have less room to play with in union he could still cause havoc. Had a brief spell with Bath where he took too many cheap shots at the bottom of rucks for his liking.

Centre – Gary Connolly

On the RFU's hit list until he signed a new contract with Wigan. Proved in his short time with Harlequins he would be able to master union given the time. Strong, skilful and a brilliant tackler, he was let down at The Stoop by Quins' inability to defend as a unit. Even stepped into the breach as goal-kicker when Andy Farrell was injured.

Centre – Kevin Iro

The beast. Powerful New Zealander who even the All Blacks must have viewed jealously as he swept all before him at Leeds. Still a threat as he proved by helping the Kiwis send Australia to a shock defeat in 1998 and turning on the power for St Helens in 1999.

Left wing – Alan Hunte

Quick, strong and an excellent finisher. His assets make him an ideal winger who would shine in a good union side. Another whom the RFU fancied the look of until they realized the state of their bank balance.

Stand-off – Michael Hagan

Another one off Australia's production line. Quite simply the best footballer I ever had the honour of playing alongside. I would bring him out of retirement to spark the backs like he did for Halifax during his time in England.

Scrum-half – Ricky Stuart

A former union scrum-half which gives him a head start, bearing in mind the differences between the two roles in the two codes. Good footballer and organizer who has starred in Kangaroo colours and would no doubt do the same in my team.

Tight-head prop – David Young

Experienced in both codes. Tough, durable and would give some semblance of order to a novice scrummaging unit. Been around a long time and has survived the ravages of the front row well enough to still be in the Wales side 12 years after his debut.

Hooker – Bobbie Goulding

Chosen on the grounds that he would hate being hooker. He just would not stop moaning. Bobbie is keen to try union and thinks he would be a big success but a few games in the front row should put him off. He would be fighting in minutes.

Loose-head prop – George Graham

Another man who knows both games. A good player for Newcastle and Scotland, particularly in the loose, who encouraged me to issue on-field bollockings to him to keep him going. His comeback to union scrummaging left him seeing stars after the first session but he gradually re-adapted.

Second row – John Harrison

The former St Helens giant earns a slot simply because he is tall – 6ft 10in. He earned a name for himself in league by heading the ball to set up tries, a tactic outlawed shortly afterwards. I'm not sure if he could get away with the same trick in union. That might be the only eventuality the law book doesn't cater for.

Second row – Karl Harrison

This position serves my good mate Rhino, with whom I spent many happy seasons at Halifax, right. It would really make him graft. Rucking, mauling and pushing in scrums would all be tasks he wasn't used to. The question is will anybody be able to lift his vast frame at lineout time?

Blind-side flanker – Andy Farrell

Excellent ball-player who would have the opportunity to run with the ball at No. 6 although his wide-ranging skills mean he could fit in almost anywhere. Missed his first Super League game in 1999 which just shows his indestructibility in what is a punishing sport. Good goalkicker too which is essential to a successful union team.

Open-side flanker – Apollo Perelini

The hardest of the lot. A former union player, it is a surprise he has not returned as yet. The only doubt would be whether his mobility has suffered because of his increase in size since he switched. Another of those God-fearing South Sea Islanders who seem to leave their peaceful side behind when they step on to a rugby pitch.

No. 8 – Barrie-Jon Mather

Tall, rangy individual with experience of Australian RL and the height to be of use at the lineout. Played international schoolboy rugby union in the pack while at Arnold School where he regularly played in the back row. I don't suppose he would fancy forward duties too much now though having seen how the other half live outside. Impressed Clive Woodward enough to make his England debut at a time when he could not get into the Sale team.

When it comes to a collection of union players capable of playing league, the selectors do not have to think beyond the All Blacks. All their players have the ball skills to slot into the league game easily. They suffered a blip in 1998 because of the loss of some of their experienced players like Frank Bunce and Zinzan Brooke but they are just a production line of talent. For me those two would be wonderful additions to any league team. Bunce plays a hard-running league-style game anyway and Brooke, who almost signed for Manly in his younger days, would be a wonderful distributor.

The Australian back division, which uses a lot of league moves, are equally capable of making the change. It would be hard to find a better pair of wings than Joe Roff and Ben Tune or a more accomplished midfield player than Tim Horan. It would be interesting too to see some of the powerful South Africans like the giant Springbok prop Os du Randt doing some damage at Knowsley Road. He is Steve Pitchford reincarnated. The South African stand-off Henry Honiball has a style which reminds me of the way Tony Myler used to dictate the play for Widnes. With a limit of four non-EU players there is no place for Va'aiga Tuigamala in my team – I wouldn't mind him as a replacement though.

Of the England squad Will Greenwood, a Blackburn lad, could make a fine rugby league player as could Tim Stimpson. Jerry Guscott would do too if he was prepared to put up with the drop in class and wages. When Jerry refused to play in the Bath v. Wigan challenge my reaction was similar to a lot of people's – the big, soft Jessie. However, having had the chance to play alongside him I have found out just how far from the truth my assessment was. Jerry is an extremely physical player who would certainly be hard enough for league. He is a clear thinker and forthright in what he wants and does not want. He decided the Bath v. Wigan matches were stunts and therefore not for him. That's Jerry for you. He does what he wants when he wants.

Some of the big names who have represented England alongside him through the years would simply not have been tough enough. Players need fighting spirit surging through their veins to make it at league and people like Rob Andrew and Rory Underwood did not have it. They were quite happy to be put up on their pedestal with England rather than get their knees dirty week in week out. They did not have the streetfighter mentality of players like Neil Jenkins, who almost signed for Sheffield Eagles once upon a time, or Gary Armstrong, both of whom were close to selection for my dream team but just missed out. Of those that did make it only three have played the game before but the rest have the talent – and the attitude – to make the transition.

Union XIII

Full-back – Alan Tait
A proven track record with Widnes and Leeds before returning to union. He has the vision to play the game from full-back, comes into the line well at pace and is a good last-man defender – except when Martin Offiah left him standing on his 90-yard run in the Challenge Cup final. His organizational skills and pace are second to none as well.

Right wing – David Campese
Fantastic entertainer. Almost impossible to defend against because you never know what is coming next. Beautifully balanced runner and, as his record suggests, a great finisher. The subject of many offers to switch codes back in Australia but having had experience of the Italian version of amateur rugby union he probably did not think it would be worth it.

Centre – Scott Gibbs
Robust defensive player who was effective during his time at St Helens and makes no secret of his liking for league.

Fringes on being dirty which is what you need in a team if you are going to be feared. Brave, honest and a good ball-handler. His performances in South Africa with the Lions were stunning as was his timing at Wembley when he denied England the last Five Nations Championship with his injury-time try.

Centre – Allan Bateman

Fast, unselfish but with an eye for the try-line. Like Gibbs, defensively sound. 'Batman' was never a massive name during his time in league with Warrington and Cronulla but has blossomed since into a top player who never takes a wrong option. Extremely unlucky to be stuck behind Gibbs and Guscott in the centre queue on the Lions tour.

Left wing – Jonah Lomu

His gigantic presence would guarantee big crowds and concentrate opposition minds. Another freak, whose size and style lend themselves perfectly to league. The All Blacks use him all over the pitch and I can see him cropping up and causing havoc in league where there is more space to exploit. Not that he needs it as he tends to just bulldoze through people anyway.

Stand-off – Carlos Spencer

A fantastic ball-handler and all-round footballer. A more talented player than Andrew Mehrtens who has kept him out of the All Blacks side in the past. I told him on the pitch during his virtuoso exhibition for the 1997 New Zealand tourists against England A at Huddersfield that he should be playing up at Headingley. Just the sort of player whose individual skills would shine through in league.

Scrum-half – Austin Healey

Like Paul Bishop, very busy and annoying. A feisty competitor who has the pace of a winger and an aggressive attitude which got him a lengthy ban for trampling on the face of London Irish's Kevin Putt. Clive Woodward showed just how highly he rated him by picking him for the bench against Wales on his return with no match practice. Used to live next to Headingley during his time at poly when he turned down an offer from Leeds RL.

Prop – Steve O'Neill
Steve who? A surprise choice to some bearing in mind he does not always make the Newcastle side but a perfect league prop. Hard-working, uncompromising and willing to put in the hard yards for the team. Gateshead Thunder wanted him on board as a local presence in their team of Australians.

Hooker – Neil Back
Tremendous work rate and good distribution skills would make him a big hit in league. He would also find some players his own size which would make a nice change for him. There was a question mark over his defence but that has been put to rest by his recent performances which make it all the more difficult to understand why England never picked him before the Woodward era.

Prop – Tim Rodber
Destructive defender who would be well suited to taking the ball up for the team with his 6-ft-6-in, 18-stone frame. Used to doing the donkey work now that he has been converted to a union second row. Not many army officers play the game but the 'Brigadier' would command respect by his performances rather than his rank.

Second row – Richard Hill
Strong, hard tackler with good ball skills and very much an

unsung hero of the England pack. Another Lion who never flinches in the close-quarters work but has the pace to get him around the field. A natural at rugby league even though he was born in Surrey.

Second row – Lawrence Dallaglio
Ditto. Hard as nails. If the RFU had wanted to give him a life ban for his contribution to *News of the World* sales, he could have made an instant transition to league. One of England's world-class players and potentially Ampleforth's first RL star.

Loose forward – Pat Lam
A massive performer for Newcastle and Northampton and a proud leader of Western Samoa. Fast and physical with a nose for the try-line, he would be another successful recruit from the islands for rugby league. A good friend of Va'aiga Tuigamala's, he could break the news to him that he isn't in the team.

These matches might go some way to breaking down the remaining barriers between league and union. What would really crack them though would be a beer-laden bonding session on a rugby tour. I feel it is my duty to use what experience I have of the social side of rugby to put out a team of cross-code ambassadors for the oval-ball game. To qualify the players selected do not have to be particularly good at either code, just excellent tourists. There are many fine players who haven't made it to the top because they messed around too much but the list I have come up with are skilful enough to have been able to compete at the highest level as well as being party-goers. A talent in itself.

Union has, or had, the reputation of being the haven for great tourists, what with Colin Smart wolfing down a bottle of after-shave after the France v. England match in Paris a few years ago, but league has managed a presence too in what I consider to be a world-beating side. The squad would have British Lions physio Mark Davies along with them to help out with any injuries like drinker's elbow – a complaint he should, by rights, suffer from badly. This mouthwatering side would be coached and managed by me. I'm not missing this trip for the world.

John Bentley's Touring Specialist XV

Full-back – Gary Connolly (Wigan RL)
A class act in both codes and not a bad rugby player either. 'Lager', as he was nicknamed during his spell at Harlequins, proved his ability to adapt to different conditions during his stint at The Stoop. A publican's son, appropriately.

Right wing – Graeme Hallas (Hull Sharks RL)
Excellent company and, belying the image of dour, stereotypical Yorkshiremen, one of several players from God's own county in the side. He wouldn't get away with any lengthy toilet trips in training with me in charge.

Centre – Dave Irwin (Ulster and Ireland)
Hard-tackling centre who took me under his wing and led me astray at sevens, county and international level. He was a doctor but like many of them ignored the damage to his liver incurred during our drinking sessions. Just the sort of bloke top-level rugby union will miss now that it has gone full-time professional.

Centre – Bryan Barley (Wakefield and England)
Sprang to notoriety on the 1988 Australia tour, up until when I had thought of him a nice reserved family man who sold

insurance. Picked up a nasty lovebite in a wrestling match with me by the swimming pool on that tour.

Left wing – Simon Irving (Leeds RL and England B)
The player with whom I have shared more beer than any other. Still comes to the annual Bentley bonfire for a can or two every 5 November, although we both have family responsibilities to ignore these days.

Stand-off – Stuart Barnes (Sky TV and the Daily Telegraph*)*
First got to know this reprobate when he was playing for the Irish Wolfhounds in the Hong Kong Sevens. He carried a crate of Bailey's around with him wherever he went. He's graduated to red wine now.

Scrum-half – Bobbie Goulding (Huddersfield RL and Great Britain)
A potential liability who will have to be kept under strict control. Always willing to follow the scent of ale; helped celebrate my first Great Britain cap in France.

Prop – Paul Rendall (Wasps and England)
The judge. A fantastic character who used to chair all England's court sessions. Knocked me back down to earth after my international call-up on the 1988 Australia tour by having me tied to a tree.

Hooker – Jon Hamer (Bradford Northern RL)
A good Yorkshire lad who played for Bradford for 10 years before their transformation into the Bulls. We're peas from the same pod. Our wives went away on holiday together with the kids, which led to a couple of savage benders for the boys left behind.

Prop – Nick Popplewell (Newcastle and Ireland)
Extremely dry sense of humour but a bit grumpy which

should add some sparks to the touring party. Great bloke and not a bad cook so he can be in charge of breakfasts.

Second row – Willie Anderson (Ulster and Ireland)
Yet another Irishman who used to make those Yorkshire v. Ulster matches so memorable. Arrested in Argentina once for pinching a national flag around the time of the Falklands War.

Second row – Steve Bainbridge (Gosforth and England, when not suspended)
Terrible disciplinary record but an entertaining character who once spilt his flaming sambuca after an England B match and set his tie on fire. The individual I would expect to be most cut up about missing the professional era, I would have him sharing rooms with Bobbie just to see what happens.

Blind-side flanker – Andy Robinson (Bath and England)
A member of the famed 7 o'clock club on the 1988 Australian tour – there were six of us and that's what time in the morning we returned after a night out. Strangely, his rugby improved while mine went downhill. Not really big enough for the No. 6 jersey but who's going to bother looking at the tour results?

Open-side flanker – Gary Rees (Nottingham and England)
Another Jack – as in 'I'm alright Jack'. Relentless ball killer who used to take some severe kickings for his troubles. Does not say much but an ever-present at the bar. Ultra-reliable and always there for you which is what you need in a tourist.

No. 8 – Lawrence Dallaglio (Wasps and England)
First ran into him on the Lions tour where we were never far apart doing the social rounds. Drinks anything – as long as it is wet and cold – but knows when and where to do it although

obviously not whom to tell about it. An inspirational leader for any tour party, I would refuse to accept his resignation from the captaincy whatever the circumstances.

Replacements

Benny Elias (Balmain and Australia RL)
Stocky drinker who proved his versatility by destroying me in places as far apart as the Gold Coast in Australia and in The Commercial in Cleckheaton.

Martin Whitcombe (Sale and England B)
An animal.

We might lose the odd game but in the after-match festivities there could be only one be winner. I would expect a lot of trouble from this tour party and it would be a difficult job for me as tour coach/manager to keep control. In fact I'd probably have to give up and muck in with them.

You can't have a tour without a few practical jokes. Hotels are a guaranteed source of fun. Piling all the charges on to the bill of a pair of room-mates is a regular winner and I would expect our team to come up trumps on this score. When it comes to check-out time it's always good to see the couple of dumb forwards who have been picked on to receive the £600 tab for champagne and strawberries argue amongst themselves over who was responsible. Removing beds from a room is another useful skill to acquire. At my Cleckheaton welcome-home dinner after the Lions tour I couldn't miss the opportunity to set up a couple of the club's old boys. They went to their room after a lovely evening only to discover their beds had disappeared so they had to sleep on the floor. I returned them in the morning.

Cars are always a favourite too. Soon after the Super

League loyalty bonuses had been paid out a few players had a lot of spare money and some of them decided to invest in cars. Bobbie Goulding was one of them. We were both picked in the England rugby league side to play Wales which meant a long journey down to Newport. We all travelled down on the bus except for Bobbie who turned up in a brand new Saab convertible. He had only driven down in it to show the thing off and he loved it. He parked it up, alarmed it and kept checking on it. You could see him sleeping in it instead of his hotel room, he was that proud. He showed it a bit more respect than Doug Laughton's car!

While we were having our evening meal, I sneaked out and asked for his room key at reception. Foolishly they gave me it and I went into his room and took his car keys. I got into Bobbie's car, and with some help from the porter, I put it in one of the hotel garages. Then I returned to dinner. I told a few of the lads and watched on in amusement as Bobbie went to check on his car only to find out it had disappeared. He went frantic. He was running around the foyer telling everyone it had been pinched and demanding that the police were called. Because of his obvious distress and the fact that there was an international next day, I let him know what had happened before the team management found out. He was very relieved although not that pleased. 'You bastard, Bentos,' he said. Not the only time I heard those words from Bobbie.

I also try never to miss a chance when it comes to a changing room prank. I use people's towels and put them back wet, nick players' boots at training or fill them with shampoo. Jockstraps too have been found lined with Deep Heat. Nick Fozzard, the Huddersfield prop, was very proud of his pristine white trainers so of course at training I went into his kitbag and swapped them for an appalling pair of mine which I use for gardening.

There are a lot of mundane duties about being a professional – it is rehearsing endlessly to make sure simple things work to perfection on the day. In the process of repetition things can become boring and these sort of things help to break the monotony. Aside from the drinking, which doesn't fit in too well with professional sport, I have always found the odd prank helpful. To be honest I can't help myself.

If you are planning a prank it is important to identify the correct victim. I like to know the person I am winding up so I can be sure of their reaction. It needs to be someone with a good sense of humour who can laugh at themselves. I also find it helpful to go for someone who is an integral part of the team, of whom some of the younger players might be wary. Respect should only stretch so far.

Humour is important within a strict environment. There is a fine line between having a laugh and things getting out of hand, of course, but a few giggles never did anyone any harm. The management, even at professional rugby clubs, tend to turn a blind eye to the goings-on because it is good for team spirit. When a team goes away on long journeys it can be like a group of schoolkids on an outing and I would expect plenty of juvenile behaviour from my line-up. Having had some experience in this field, my tourists would be hard-pressed to get one over on their coach/manager. After all, you can't kid the kid who's kidded everyone.

Chapter 12

So which is the better game? I have played in some great matches in both codes and I have watched crackers in both too. For the past few years I have alternated between the two, which in hindsight is not something I would recommend to every player for the sake of your mind as much as your body. Not having a break is exhausting mentally. But as a winger it is possible and from my stand-point, out on the touchline, I prefer to play rugby league because I am always involved.

I have played in quite a few union games where I only touched the ball two or three times. This lack of involvement, even in the improved modern game, meant I would come off the pitch feeling I still had plenty in reserve which was frustrating. It wasn't a deliberate decision but I became lazier as a result in my attitude to training in the winter as opposed to the summer when my fitness levels needed to be at their highest.

The chance to shine in defeat was a noticeable difference from union, in that you were guaranteed a certain amount of possession in league to do something with. In union if your forwards cannot win enough ball there isn't much you can do about it except settle down for an afternoon of tackling.

I am sure if you talk to any of the union players who went across to league they will tell you how much better they became as a result. They came for the money but went away with a liking for the sport itself. A lot would play league again tomorrow if the money was right. In many ways league represents union 100 years on. When the Northern Union broke away in 1895 they were playing exactly the same sports. The only difference was in allowing broken-time payments. League developed the way it did to try to improve the spectacle and attract people to watch the game and pay the bills. Now union has some pretty hefty bills of its own to pay it will be interesting to see how far down it goes along the same route.

Union players are bulking themselves up and wearing league-style padding too so they are beginning to look similar. The rules on protection, like many other things, remain all over the place after the hasty transition from amateurism. For some reason Premiership players are not allowed to wear the same padding as those taking part in internationals. I ended up hiding from referees and touch judges when they came into the changing room so they could not check my padded vest but when they caught me out I had to take it off on the field during matches.

In a sense the theory behind the two codes is converging too. In union the aim is no longer to score as quickly as possible but to keep possession for phase after phase until the perfect chance appears. Possession is becoming guaranteed so long as you have the building blocks within the side to supply it in the first place and that is changing the game beyond all recognition. If your side does not make a mistake, it is extremely hard for the opposition to get hold of the ball.

The aim is to create a better spectacle. Teams who kick penalties to touch now win the lineout throw and with lifting allowed they are virtually guaranteed the ball. So teams have to keep control of the ball instead of hoofing it into the stand because if they do so they are almost certainly giving away possession. The chaos at rucks has also been cleaned up because sides are not committing as many players to them. The days of diving in and killing the ball are almost over at top level as sides remain intent on building a defensive wall across the field. Opponents are being allowed the ball on the ground but challenged harder in the tackle instead. This is an interesting development in itself because it has led to league techniques being employed to try to free up the ball in the tackle.

Changing the law to ensure the back rows remain bound at the scrum has also opened up rugby union enormously. The extra space on the field means tries can now be scored from first-phase possession and union is a better game for it.

A couple of seasons ago when the Northampton played Newcastle in a televised Tetley's Bitter Cup tie on the same afternoon as St Helens v. Warrington, I chose the union game to watch. That says a lot about how union has developed and also something about the fact that Sandy put her foot down about watching two matches in one day!

Professionalism may have brought an improved spectacle and standard of play but it has been a painful revolution for rugby union. In the end I think there will be a breakaway in club rugby union. Not the top clubs leaving the Rugby Football Union as many people predicted but a breakaway in the other direction by the smaller clubs. Soon they will decide it is time to step back. Those that are trying desperately to embrace professionalism as best they can will see the wisdom in returning to the old days of social rugby and leaving the big boys and the ambitious, well-financed sides like Worcester to it. They would be wise to do so. The mass stampede to professionalism has not claimed all of its victims yet.

The ultimate goal for northern hemisphere rugby union has to be a 12- or 14-club European League which will provide an equivalent to the Super-12s. There will be losers from this streamlining and the owners whose clubs miss out might leave the game but this sort of elite competition is what is needed. The structure is there already, all rugby union has to do is use it.

While union has changed to provide the entertainment that rugby league used to supply, my fear is that the 13-man code is aping the type of game that was being played in Australia five years ago. It is a defence-orientated brand of rugby league built on players whose size has increased markedly courtesy of a lot of weight-training. A decade ago you could guarantee sides would have a hole or two to exploit in the English game – there are no weak links in Super League now. Somehow more attention has to be paid to improving attacking methods otherwise there is a danger that defence will dominate too much.

Some of rugby league's rule changes, brought in to improve the game, have been misguided. For instance players used to be allowed to steal a ball in the tackle. It didn't matter how many tacklers were involved – they could all join in. But the rule-makers outlawed ball-stripping only to bring it back in a confusing form which allowed possession to be stolen when just one tackler was involved. This led to a lot of marginal decisions. Another about-turn happened with the kick-off. The side who scored the try was awarded the kick-off in 1998 before they reverted back to the traditional method the following season. It seemed to be change for change's sake.

One alteration I did like was the introduction of the 40/20 rule which allows a side to regain possession if they bounce the ball into touch inside the opponents' 20-metre line with a kick from outside their own 40-metre line. It really keeps the wingers on their toes. They have to be up for the tackle but aware of the increased likelihood of a kick. If a side has a good kicker to exploit the rule, the tactic can be used as an important weapon and it helps to make the game less predictable. Teams were putting so much emphasis on keeping the ball in the early tackles that sides had become very conservative. Risks were only being taken towards the end of the six tackles in case they lost possession.

The increase in the number of substitutions was a good move too, particularly for sweaty summer rugby. That helps to give extra breathers to players although a side-effect was to benefit the bigger clubs who can afford better squads. I would like to see things changed further to bring in unlimited substitutions like in Australia.

There are other good changes which have had unfortunate side-effects. Although doubling the distance a defence had to retreat at the play-the-ball to 10 metres created more space for the attacking side it inadvertently killed off the skilful prop. Nowadays there is no one to take the place of ball-players like Lee Crooks and Kevin Ward who had to open up defences through sleight of hand from close range as well as batter through them. All you need now is a tank in your No. 10 shirt.

In televised games the referee now has the choice of using the fourth official who has access to video tapes of the action. If the technology is available it should be used as it has helped to get more decisions right. However as a player it does become a pain if the official causes a delay by replaying the incident time and again before making his call.

For referees and players the introduction of the sin-bin has been brilliant. As sure as fish swim, rugby players cheat and if the option is there to stop professional fouls it has to be applauded. Previously players knew they could get away with lying-on at the tackle without any chance of them being dismissed but now they have to think twice. However what has been used as a cop-out by officials is the business of sin-binning a player and putting them on report for offences that warrant instant dismissal. If players commit a sending-off offence, they should be sent off. It's as simple as that.

Despite its mixed record with rule changes league just about has the game at the moment while union undoubtedly has the occasion. There is absolutely nothing in league, save maybe the Challenge Cup final, that is a patch on the international days union can provide. And on the international occasions when union produces total rugby, like when England drew with New Zealand at Twickenham in December 1997, there is really only one winner. That match touched on the type of rugby the Lions were playing in South Africa – the most intense, high-profile rugby of either code I have ever experienced.

Union is well on the way to catching up, and in some cases, surpassing league in terms of professionalism and it has access to some extremely wealthy backers. If league is not careful, it will become a feeder game for union. Professionalism has already halted the flow of top rugby union players to league and as it develops I can see the situation happening in reverse. The best league players are now fair game for union to snap up. The league clubs are not daft – they will try to keep them in contract – but the lure of the international stage and World Cups may prove too strong to resist for these boys. I would not be surprised to see some major transfers from league to union in the near future. Of course there is no guarantee these players will make it. Tulsen Tollett, Graeme Hallas and Mike Forshaw, all good league players, were not up to the standard demanded by Harlequins and Saracens but the real cream like Gary Connolly and Jason Robinson would make fantastic union players.

Rugby union has been guilty of looking down its nose at rugby league in the past but I don't believe it does these days. The players have never been the problem – my old North teammates used to bend their noses across their faces and shout 'come short' when they saw me after my switch of codes but it was teasing born out of respect for a hard game. In the north rugby people from either code live shoulder to shoulder without many problems, taking an interest in each others' games. However in the south of England where people have had very little exposure to league, snobbery is harder to wipe out. This is particularly true of the London-based national press where games that attract much bigger crowds than their union counterparts receive virtually no coverage. Perhaps they judge the 'wrong' sort of people are at the games.

Having had a century of being sneered at, league has found it difficult to suddenly accept the hand of friendship now union has followed the same path and gone professional. Shoulders are covered in chips from Post Office Road to the Boulevard. There are still many league people who suffer from such bad inverted snobbery that when England play at rugby union they automatically support the opposition. They are not sure whether to poke fun at union for coming to league for knowledge and players, or to worry that their game could have its best assets stripped.

This antipathy is one reason why I doubt there will ever be one game of rugby, taking the best of both codes. The only way it will come about is if a television mogul like Rupert Murdoch or Kerry Packer demanded it with massive financial backing. Money talks and if Murdoch bought up 250 players to represent 10 franchises around England then it could happen. Television drives both games now and those who believe otherwise are living in a fool's paradise. We are all in the entertainment business. However I cannot see how Murdoch would benefit from merging the codes. Nor do I swallow the global conspiracy theory that has Murdoch wanting to control a new world sport which incorporates league, union and American Football. He has what he wants. His investment in league means he has a live summer game to fill Sky airtime with while his union deal gives him the same in winter.

Even if the unthinkable did happen at the top, union and league would continue to exist at grassroots level in their regional strongholds. I mean rugby league in Gloucester and rugby union in Featherstone – it's just not right is it?

I can't see rugby challenging soccer in terms of crowds or interest even if there were a merger at top level. Super League officials get excited when Bradford and Leeds draw 21,000 as does the English First Division when Saracens and Leicester reach five figures. But the crowds are still less than half those that the top soccer clubs draw every week.

The two codes are probably best off ploughing their own separate furrows and serving their own constituencies. Now league has moved to summer there is no reason why they cannot co-exist quite happily. Both have a lot to offer, both are great games. I owe them everything.

Epilogue

....

A small piece of advice

There once was a bird flying along in the middle of winter. Tired and bedraggled, it was overcome by the cold and the wind chill and it fell to the ground. As it lay in the grass, shivering and preparing to breathe its last, a cow walked by and dropped a hefty load of hot manure on it. This revived the bird and it soon came fully back to life and began to sing merrily. The noise alerted the attention of a nearby cat which pulled the bird out of the manure and ate it.

The moral of my story is as follows: not everybody who shits on you is your enemy; not everybody who pulls you out of the shit is your friend; but if you're in the shit and you're happy keep your mouth shut.

Keep smiling,
John Bentley

Appendix

....

John Bentley's career statistics

Season	Club	Appearances	Tries	Goals
1985–6	Otley	26	14	1
1986–7	Otley	20	16	10
	Yorkshire	8	5	
1987–8	Sale	30	16	
	Yorkshire	6	6	1
1988–9	Sale	8	2	1
	Yorkshire	4	0	
	Leeds RL	21	15	12
1989–90	Leeds RL	20 + 3	10	15
1990–1	Leeds RL	21 + 3	9	
1991–2	Leeds RL	30 + 3	19	
1992–3	Halifax RL	29	20	
1993–4	Halifax RL	32	25	
	Balmain Tigers RL	11	1	
1994–5	Halifax RL	33	29	
1995–6	Halifax RL	12	10	
1996	Halifax RL	20 + 1	22	
1996–7	Newcastle	17 + 1	23	
1997	Halifax RL	2	0	
1997–8	Newcastle	6 + 1	3	
	Rotherham	7	1	
1998	Halifax RL	4 + 2	3	
1999	Huddersfield RL			

International career

Date	Opponents	Result	Tries
England			
23 April 1988	v. Ireland (Dublin)	W 21–10	0
29 May 1988	v. Australia (Brisbane)	L 16–22	1
12 July 1997	v. Australia (Sydney)	L 6–25	0
29 November 1997	v. South Africa (Twickenham)	L 11–29	0
British Lions 1997 to South Africa			
28 May	v. Border (East London)	W 18–14	1
31 May	v. Western Province (Cape Town)	W 38–21	2
7 June	v. Northern Transvaal (Pretoria)	L 30–35	0
11 June	v. Gauteng (Johnnesburg)	W 20–14	1
17 June	v. Emerging Springboks (Wellington)	W 51–22	0
24 June	v. Free State (Bloemfontein)	W 52–30	3
28 June	v. South Africa (2nd Test, Durban)	W 25–16	0
5 July	v. South Africa (3rd Test, Jo'burg)	L 35–16	0
England RL			
15 February 1995	v. France (Gateshead)	W 19–15	0
7 October 1995	v. Australia (Wembley)	W 20–16	0
11 October 1995	v. Fiji (Wigan)	W 46–0	1
14 October 1995	v. South Africa (Headingley)	W 46–0	0
26 June 1996	v. Wales (Cardiff Arms Park)	W 26–12	0
Great Britain RL			
16 February 1992	v. France (Perpignan)	W 30–12	1
20 March 1994	v. France (Carcassonne)	W 12–4	0

Index

··

Agar, Alan 102
aggression, on pitch 65
All Blacks (RU)
    game skills 210-11
    v Emerging England 190
Anderson, Willie 218
Andrew, Rob 38, 47, 129, 134-5,
    186-9
Archer, Gareth 134, 135
attitudes
    discipline 16-17
    drugs 173
    race 13
Austin, Greg 105
Australia (RL)
    v Great Britain 114, 115
    v Halifax 107
Australia (RU), v England 49-50,
    51, 181-2
Australians, playing style 110

Back, Neil 214
Bainbridge, Steve 44, 218
Baird, Roger 30
Baldwin, Simon 118, 122
Balmain Tigers (RL) 109, 111-13
    v Gold Coast 112
    v St George 112
Barley, Bryan 216-17
Barnes, Stuart 217
Bateman, Allan 213
Bath (RU), v Wigan (RL) 206
Bayfield, Martin 85
Bentley, Faye (daughter) 100, 126-7
Bentley, John

attitudes 13, 16-17, 173
character 4-6, 7-8, 106-7, 134,
    186, 219-21
childhood 11-17
code change 2, 55-7
cross-code playing 20-21
education 14, 16-17, 20
other sports 21-2
other work 58-9, 83-92, 118
parents 17, 46, 149-50
rugby league
    clubs see Balmain Tigers;
    Dewsbury Moor; Halifax;
    Huddersfield; Leeds
    internationals see Great
    Britain
rugby union
    clubs see Cleckheaton;
    Huddersfield; Newcastle;
    Otley; Rotherham; Sale
    internationals see British
    Lions; Emerging England;
    England; England B; England
    Colts
    regional see Northern;
    Yorkshire
Sandy
    engagement 52-4
    marriage 125
Bentley, Lloyd (son) 19, 126
Bentley, Millie (daughter) 125, 127
Bentley (parents) 17, 46, 149-50
Bentley, Sandy (wife) 29, 99-100,
    140
    engagement 52-4

Bentley, Sandy (wife) *cont.*
  first meeting 37-8
  marriage 125
  pregnancies 125-7
Bentley, Sarah (sister) 14-15
Betts, Denis 114, 164
Bishop, Paul 98
Black, Steve 131-2
Bradford Bulls 120-21
British Lions (RU)
  South African tour 2, 139, 147-8,
    150-51, 173-8
    captaincy 141
    entertainments officer 151-3
    media attention 178-9
    players 144-6
    selection for 142-3
    substitute 165-6
    Test Matches 4, 165-6, 167-
      70, 177
    v Free State 4, 177
    v Gauteng Lions 148-9, 161-3
Broomhead, Joe 19
Butterfield, Bob 19

Campese, David 49, 212
Canada (RU), England Colts tour
  35-6
captaincy, Halifax 105, 106-7
Carling, Will 7, 23, 24, 26, 178
  England team 45, 47
Catt, Mike 162
character
  exhibitionist 6-7
  practical joker 5, 7-8, 106-7, 134,
    219-21
  unpredictability 5-6, 186
  work ethic 4
childhood
  fears 13-14
  Liversedge 14-16
  South Africa 11-13
children, involvement in sport 110
Clarke, Phil 114
Cleckheaton (RU) 17-18, 20, 33-4, 37
Connolly, Gary 208, 216
Cooke, Geoff 24-5, 26, 46, 50-51
Cotton, Fran 3-4, 38, 55-6, 139, 142

Coventry (RU), v Newcastle 156
cricket 21-2
Crooks, Lee 61
cross-code
  dream teams 207-15
  matches 205-7
  playing 2, 128-9, 184
cross-country running 22
crowd abuse 64-5

Dallaglio, Lawrence 170-73, 215,
  218-19
Davidson, Jeremy 168
Davies, Alan 44
Davies, Jonathan 68-9, 104
Davies, Phil 85
de Glanville, Phil 141, 182-3
Delaney, Paul 72
Devereux, John 67, 68
Dewsbury Moor (RL) 20-21, 29
Divorty, Gary 77, 98, 164
Dooley, Wade 45
Dracup, James 28
dream teams
  cross-code 216-19
  league playing union 207-10
  touring 216-19
  union playing league 210-12
drug-taking 170-73
Dudley, John 34
Durham (RU), v Yorkshire 23-4,
  164

Edwards, Shaun 105
Elias, Benny 109, 219
Ellis, St John 77, 108
Emerging England (RU), v All
  Blacks 190
England B (RU)
  v France 44-5
  v Spain 44
England Colts (RU)
  Canada tour 35-6
  internationals 35
  trial 34-5
England (RU)
  Five Nations 192
  training 1980s 48-9

trial 43-4
v Australia 49-50, 51, 181-2
v Ireland 46-7
v South Africa 191-2
Evans, Ieuan 7, 166-7

Fallon, Jim 75
Farrell, Andy 210
Fiji (RL), v Great Britain 114
Finn, Brendan 102
fitness
    Newcastle Falcons (RU) 131-2
    rugby league 60-61
Fleming, Dave 99
Ford, Phil 58, 74
France (RL), v Great Britain 77-8,
    104
France (RU), v England B 44-5

Gallagher, John 70-71
Garforth, Darren 184
Gartland, Tony 117-18
Gibbs, Scott 146, 152, 157, 212-13
goalkicking
    abilities 31
    specialists 167-8
Gosforth (RU), v Otley 29
Goulding, Bobby 73, 78, 203, 209,
    217
Graham, George 133, 209
Great Britain (RL)
    declines New Zealand tour 130
    v Australia 114, 115
    v Fiji 114
    v France 77-8, 104
    v South Africa 114
    Wigan contingent 105
    World Cup 1995 113-15
    World Sevens 107-9, 110
Greenwood, Will 177
Guscott, Jeremy 6, 144-5, 152, 168,
    169, 211

Hagan, Michael 104, 208
Halifax (RL)
    Blue Sox 121
    British Lions tour 139-40
    captaincy 105, 106

changes at 117-18
contract 118-19
deal with Newcastle 130
following 97
return to 198-9
transfer to 76-7, 97-8
v Australia 107
v Huddersfield 105-6
v Leeds 74, 100
v London Broncos 127
v Sheffield Eagles 155-6
v Warrington 163
v Wigan 100-1, 105
World Club Championship 184-5
Hall, Sir John 129-30, 136, 186
Hallas, Graeme 100, 103-4, 216
Halliday, Simon 47
Hamer, Jon 217
Hanley, Ellery 71-2, 107
Harrison, John 209
Harrison, Karl 105, 107, 117
Harrison, Mike 24, 30, 46, 164
Headingley (RU) 27-8
    v Sale 40-41
Headlands Junior School 16-17, 20
Healey, Austin 213-14
Heckmondwike Grammar School
    20
Hendriks, Pieter 161
Heslop, Nigel 32
Hill, Richard 214-15
Hogg, Rod 34
Hong Kong Sevens 52-3
Howe, John 41
Huddersfield (RL) 199-202
    Halifax 105-6
Hull Kingston Rovers (RL) 56-7
Hunte, Alan 208

injuries
    'ankle' 98-9
    broken noses 21-2, 31, 78
    cheekbone 99
    foot 198
    hamstring 114
    knee 198
    neck 92-3
    ribs 185

injuries *cont.*
   shoulder 36
   toe 151
International Rugby Board 117
Ireland (RU), v England 46-7
Iro, Kevin 208
Irving, Simon 19, 33, 40-41, 217

Jenkins, Neil 162, 167, 169
Johnson, Martin 140-42

Kebbie, Birmah 56, 164
Kelso (RU), v Otley 30
Kiernan, Michael 47

Lagisquet, Patrick 44
Lam, Pat 215
Laughton, Doug 55, 56, 71, 74, 77
Leeds (RL)
   atmosphere at 58
   facilities 63-4
   signs contract 57
   status 62-3
   transfer from 75-6
   v Halifax 74, 100
   v St Helens 70, 164
   v Wakefield Trinity 70, 164
   v Warrington 70
   v Widnes 67, 68, 72-3
   v Wigan 73-4, 75, 163-4
   v York 58-9
Leonard, Jason 145, 184
Lindsay, Maurice 55, 78, 114, 123
Lomu, Jonah 190-91, 213
London Broncos (RL) 121
   v Halifax 127
Loughlin, Paul 8, 200
Lydon, Joe 101
Lynagh, Michael 49

McGeechan, Ian 3-4, 141, 142, 157-8
McVey, Derek 112
Mather, Barrie-Jon 210
Millward, Roger 101-2

New Zealand (RU) *see* All Blacks
Newcastle Falcons (RU)

approached by 129
deal with Halifax 130
dropped from team 186-8
facilities 131
team bonding 133-4
team tactics 136-7, 188-90
training 131-2
v Coventry 156
young players 193
Newlove, Paul 104, 108
North Midlands (RU), v Yorkshire 38
Northern Division (RU) 24-5
   Colts 34

Oasis 153-4
Offiah, Martin 6-7, 78, 207
   encounters with 66-7, 75, 101, 135
O'Neill, Steve 214
Otley (RU)
   Florida tour 32-3
   joins 28, 33
   v Gosforth 29
   v Kelso 30
   v Wakefield 30

Panapa, Sam 101, 163
Pearce, Gary 44
Pearce, Wayne 109, 111
Perelini, Apollo 99, 210
police 58-9, 83, 93-5
   sport 32
police career
   Halifax 91-2
   Hyde Park (Leeds) 89-90
   leaves 118
   training course 84-5
   Weetwood (Leeds) 85-9
Popplewell, Nick 129, 136, 217-18
positions (playing)
   centre 24, 33
   No.8 33-4
   scrum half 19, 33
   wing 35, 100
Powell, Roy 65-6, 67
pre-match strategies 161-2, 168-9
Preston, Mark 46, 101, 105
professionalism, defined 3, 132-3

Radlinski, Kris 207
Rees, Gary 218
Reilly, Malcolm
  Great Britain coach 78
  Halifax coach 102-4, 117
  Huddersfield coach 199-200
  Leeds coach 69, 78
Rendall, Paul 217
Richards, Dean 85
Richmond (RU) 131
Robinson, Andy 218
Robinson, Dave 44
Robinson, Jason 207-8
Roche, Alan 34
Rodber, Tim 214
Rotherham (RU) 128, 195-6
Rowell, Jack 181-2, 183
Rowley, Paul 118
Rugby Football Union 5, 183, 194-5, 197
  battle with clubs 9, 195
rugby league
  antagonism to union 59, 229
  Australia 110-11
  Challenge Cup 123-4
  club mergers 119
  comparison with union 223-4
  cross-code matches 205-7
  declines New Zealand tour 130
  first interest in 30-31
  fitness 60-61
  history 224
  influence of television 230
  opportunities for young 83
  preference for 223
  rule changes 226-8
  Sky TV 121, 122, 127, 197-8
  summer game 117, 119-20, 123-4
  Super League 120
  World Cup structure 115
  see also individual clubs
rugby union
  communication 158
  comparison with league 223-4
  cross-code matches 205-7
  drug testing 172
  European League 226
  full-backs 61

influence of television 230
internationals 5, 228
leagues introduced 43
open sport decision 117
opportunities for young 83
'payments' 1-2, 28-9, 40
professionalism 2, 27, 197-8, 225-6, 228-9
rugby league influences 2, 3-4, 184
rule changes 224-5
see also individual clubs

St Helens (RL), v Leeds 70, 164
Sale (RU) 38-40
  v Headingley 40-41
Saracens (RU) 27
Schofield, Gary 71
schools
  bullying 14
  Headlands JS 16-17, 20
  Heckmondwike GS 20
Schuster, John 104, 121
sendings-off 155-6
Sharp, Henry 75
Sheffield Eagles (RL), v Halifax 155-6
Shepherd, John 24
Simms, Steve 117, 127-8
Sironen, Paul 109
Small, James 154-5
Smallwood, Andy 156
Smith, Steve 38
Smith, Tom 145-6, 168, 184
snobbery 229-30
Sorensen, Kurt 68
South Africa (RL), v Great Britain 114
South Africa (RU)
  changes after Lions' tour 175
  foul play 156-7
  multi-racialism in 175-6
  v England 191-2
  see also British Lions
Spain (RU), v England B 44
Spencer, Carlos 213
sport, motivation 18-19
Stansfield, Phil 40

Stapleton, Danny 112
Stimpson, Tim 167, 187
Stuart, Ricky 208-9
Super League Europe 9, 120
superstition 178

Tait, Alan 30, 78-9, 133, 168, 212
television
    influence on development 230
    interviews 127
    News Corporation 123
    Sky 121, 122, 127, 197-8
Telfer, Jim 141, 142, 158-9
Tipping, Simon 39-40
touring, economics 52, 140
Townsend, Gregor 146
training
    attitude to 3
    Australia (RL) 110
    England (RU) 1980s 48-9
    Huddersfield Giants 201
    Malcolm Reilly 103-4
    Newcastle Falcons (RU) 131-2
    summer 124
    see also fitness
tries
    British Lions 148-9, 151, 161
    favourite 163-5
    hat tricks 44, 70, 166, 185
    Leeds (RL) 66, 70
    Newcastle Falcons (RU) 137
    v Gauteng Lions 161, 162-3
    v Sheffield Eagles 123
    v South Africa (RU) 1997 4-5
Tuigamala, Va'aiga 130, 133, 134-5
Twickenham 191

Umaga, Mike 121-2
Underwood, Rory, personality 38,
    50-51

Venter, Andre 155

Waddington, Simon 29
Wakefield (RU), v Otley 30
Wakefield Trinity (RL), v Leeds 70,
    164
Wallace, Paul 145-6, 184
Ward, David 69
Warrington (RL)
    v Halifax 163
    v Leeds 70
Watson, Dave 112-13
Webb, Jonathan 47
Weir, Doddie 129, 135-6, 140, 152,
    156-7
West Yorkshire Police (RU), v
    Northumbria 31-2
Whitcombe, Martin 39, 219
Whiteley, Chris 128
Widnes (RL) 55-6, 67-9
    v Leeds 67, 68, 72-3
Wigan (RL)
    v Bath (RU) 206
    v Halifax 100-1, 105
    v Leeds 73-4, 75, 163-4
Wilkinson, Jonny 193-5
Williams, Clive 34
Woodward, Clive 183-4, 190
World Club Championship (RL)
    184-5

York (RL), v Leeds 58-9
Yorkshire Cup final (RU) 31
Yorkshire (RU)
    Colts trial 34
    County Championship 1986-87
    38
    v Durham 23-4, 164
    v North Midlands 38
Young, David 209